12.60

The New Romantics

The New Romantics

A REAPPRAISAL OF THE NEW CRITICISM

RICHARD FOSTER

KENNIKAT PRESS
Port Washington, N. Y./London

THE NEW ROMANTICS

Copyright © 1962 by Indiana University Press
Published in 1973 by Kennikat Press by
arrangement with Indiana University Press
Library of Congress Catalog Card No.: 72-85288
ISBN 0-8046-1696-5

Manufactured by Taylor Publishing Company   Dallas, Texas

ACKNOWLEDGMENTS

I wish to thank the following publishers and authors for permission to quote from material under their copyrights: Harcourt, Brace & World, Inc. for R. P. Blackmur, *The Lion and the Honeycomb* and *Language as Gesture;* W. W. Norton & Company, Inc. for I. A. Richards, *Coleridge on Imagination;* Alan Swallow for Allen Tate, *The Collected Essays;* Eliseo Vivas and Farrar, Straus & Cudahy, Inc. for Eliseo Vivas, *Creation and Discovery;* University of Chicago Press for Eliseo Vivas, *The Moral Life and the Ethical Life.* I also wish to thank Wayne State University Press for giving me permission to print "Criticism as Poetry" in revised form from *Criticism,* I (Spring, 1959), and The Johns Hopkins University Press for giving me permission to reprint "The Romanticism of I. A. Richards" in revised form from *ELH,* XXVI (March, 1959), 91–101.

Contents

Preface

Now that even jokes about "criticism of criticism" have become passé, it is even more difficult than it used to be to justify still another book on modern criticism—difficult to feel confident that one's justification, persuasive in one's own eyes, will persuade others. My justification is simply that the New Criticism is a phenomenon of major importance in modern literary history, and is thus an object of continuing interest, and that what I have to say about the nature of that importance has not quite been said before in quite the ways I say it.

What if Eliot had written no criticism? What if there had been no Ransom, Tate, Richards, Brooks, Blackmur, *et al.* to irritate, with their esotericism, cultishness, jargon, and reaction, the official literary culture of their time into attention to the new writers and new modes that have since become classic? Without recent criticism —principally what is called the "New Criticism"—we would have had, I think, a different, and probably much less rich, various, and free recent literature. My view is that the New Critics and their followers and associates, by bringing an experimental underground literature above ground and giving its practice and study an urgent human importance and seriousness, created, or re-created, the dominant Anglo-American literary culture of the past half century. This book, based on that conviction, is a study of the somewhat paradoxical nature of the New Criticism, and of some of the prime attitudes, manners, and vocabularies, both conscious and unconscious, by means of which they achieved their successes.

I wish to thank Roy Harvey Pearce and Mark Spilka for making suggestions for revisions that substantially improved the book, and I am especially indebted to Walter Sutton for being a good critic and a good friend throughout its writing. I also wish to thank Bernard Schilling, Allen Tate, and I. A. Richards for kindnesses along the way. To Elizabeth Ames and the Corporation of Yaddo I am grateful for the summer of sumptuous ease during which much of the first draft was written. My thanks are also due to the McKnight Foundation for assistance in the preparation of the final manuscript, and to the editors of *Accent, Criticism, ELH, The Hudson Review,* and *The Western Review* for giving me permission to reprint here revised versions of material that originally appeared in their magazines.

RICHARD FOSTER

Minneapolis, Minnesota

PART I

Introductory

But what a relief it is not to have too many claims made for poetry.

R. P. BLACKMUR

PART 1

chapter 1

The Identity of the New Criticism

THE TERM "New Criticism" is now usually capitalized and commonly appears in the indexes and marginalia of our literary histories and survey anthologies, so one may suppose that what it designates has been generally accepted as an accomplished fact. There was once a time, say from the mid-thirties to the mid-forties, when the literary majority, then constituted by a variety of academicians and literary journalists, must have regarded it as an ephemera, a sport, or they would not have been so confident they could kill it. But it has survived, indeed it has triumphed—principally by absorbing its more numerous adversary, the professors, and leaving the relatively unrespectable journalists without either ally or adversary. The New Critics, once a tiny if truculent splinter group of what were regarded as Bohemian subversives, are now respectable and legion.

And like everything else, they have been institutionalized. Nearly every major college English department
has it share of New Critics or Younger Critics, and there
is hardly a professor any more, this side of the linguist
and bibliographer, who does not encourage skills of
"analysis" in his students and cherish notions of critical
prowess in himself.

In one of the last full-scale professorial attacks on the
New Critics, Professor Douglas Bush characterized
them, in 1949, as "a little world of several dozen people
who embody all the literary intelligence of the country,
who form a compact and exclusive communion of
saints" notable for their "agile cerebration" and "intellectual bubble-blowing." [1] If Professor Bush's view
was a bit out of date even at the time he articulated it, it
seems very much more out of date now. Putting aside
the question of respectability, the "little world of several dozen" has grown so prodigiously that it is now
almost impossible to identify the individual species *New
Critic* as something distinct from the general run of
competent literary academics.

It used to be that you could tell a New Critic by his
unfavorable attitudes toward academics on the one hand
and journalist-reviewers on the other: his "basic antagonisms," as one commentator has put it, toward "the self-
indulgence of critical impressionism" and the "academicism of university English departments." [2] The writings
of Ransom, Richards, and Brooks, certainly, often

enough exhibit these antagonisms. T. S. Eliot has said that modern criticism sprang from a discontent with the critical impressionism of thirty years ago,[3] and Allen Tate that the term *New Criticism* designates "a particular return to the literary text, along with a revolt against historical scholarship." [4] But these "antagonisms" are no longer sufficiently defining characteristics of the New Criticism, whatever they may have been some years ago. First of all, perhaps the largest share of the pieces by New Critics that have become classics of modern criticism have been "essay"—semi-poetic revery and personal impressionism—rather than "analysis." And as for the supposed anti-academicism, the fact that some of the most productive and influential scholars of recent years have also been leaders among the New Critics (men like René Wellek, Austin Warren, F. O. Matthiessen, and W. K. Wimsatt, Jr.) should sufficiently expose that oversimplification.

It was also common in the past to identify the New Criticism with a certain set of tastes or literary prejudices —or, to put it more technically, with a certain rather exclusive "theory" of literature. The New Critics were supposed to favor a highly organized and complicated poetry; a poetry that is intellectual, allusive, crotchety, packed; a poetry whose quality of ingenious if obscure coherence was named by such New Critical tags as "irony," "ambiguity," and "metaphysical." Such prescriptive tastes—and here we should once again recall

Professor Bush's accusations of literary snobbery and cultism—necessarily involved an implicit or explicit devaluation of some traditional literature. This adjustment had its beginnings in the New Critics' implicit reinstatement of Poetry in its classic position of ascendancy over other literary modes. For the New Critics tended to ignore the drama, and excepting a chosen few novelists like Henry James, Dostoievski, and James Joyce, they had very little interest in prose fiction. They were accused of a certain cultish narrowness, sometimes even of ignorance, in their tendency to exalt certain periods of literary history (notably the seventeenth and twentieth centuries) at the implicit or explicit expense of certain others (the eighteenth and nineteenth), as well as to undervalue certain classic figures in the tradition. Brooks, Richards, and Eliot had disparaged the Romantics; Eliot and Leavis attacked Milton; Ransom found Shakespeare sometimes wanting; Tate dispraised Spenser and the traditions of allegory; and nobody mentioned Chaucer. Yeats, Eliot, Stevens, Pound, and, of course, Dante and Donne—these were the poets in whose image both the poetic tastes and poetic theories of the New Critics were supposed to have been all but exclusively formed.

Yet how many exceptions to these stereotypes were ignored! I. A. Richards, for example, seemed most naturally to turn to a nineteenth-century tradition of taste when he wanted something, good or bad, to work on—the English humanist-scholar's tradition of poetry centering in Shakespeare, Milton, and the great Romantics. And Yvor Winters, the New Critic's New Critic, tended to elevate certain minor Victorian hangovers at the expense of modern deities like T. S. Eliot. Cleanth Brooks dealt kindly with Tennyson, and Eliot himself praised not only Tennyson, but also Dryden and Johnson as poets. Ransom, long an admirer of Milton, has in recent years had admiring things to say of Wordsworth as well as the other Romantics. The greatness of Keats and Coleridge has been reaffirmed many times by nearly all the exponents of New Criticism. And one must also take into account such critics as Fergusson, Wimsatt, and Heilman, all closely associated with the New Criticism proper, who have made virtual specialties, respectively, of the drama, the eighteenth century, and Shakespeare. One commentator blandly declared as late as 1954 that the New Criticism was "a movement to set up Donne and the metaphysical poets as a standard for poetry." [5] It obviously was—and is—much more than that.

There have been two other generally held defining assumptions about the nature of the New Criticism that seem to me just as narrowly inadequate as those already considered. The first of these is the assumption that the New Criticism has been an almost exclusively, and perhaps decadently, aestheticistic movement which tended to encourage a separation of literature from "life" and from the actual intellectual and spiritual problems of man individually and in society. The second assumption, which, I think, in some ways implicitly contradicts the first, is that the New Critics' theoretical opposition to romanticism makes it intellectually and temperamentally a classicistic literary movement. Putting the two assumptions together yields the interesting characterization of the New Critic as aesthetical classicist, or better, as a kind of neo-classic aesthete. These are not impossible characterizations, but I think they are reflections less of the real nature of the New Criticism than of the rather rash or muddled apprehensions of some of its opponents.

Alfred Kazin, who in the forties called for a "fresh and virile intellectual leadership" and who, after the fashion of Van Wyck Brooks, valued literature chiefly "in its relationship to life," viewed with alarm what he supposed were the bad results of the New Criticism in "a literature cut off from the main sources of life and floundering in the sick self-justification of estheticism." [6] This view, though usually less direly expressed, was the one characteristically taken during the disputative years by the assorted opposition.[7] But it is a little hard to see, from the present perspective, where very much evidence for it could be found. Perhaps the beginnings of a case could be made from the work of William Empson and Cleanth Brooks. Yet their procedures were so business-like as to cause another sort of critic to think of them as quite the reverse of aesthetes. It was their desire for precision and completeness of verbal analysis that once led Elder Olson, a Neo-Aristotelian, to complain that the " 'new criticism' . . . seems to be almost universally regarded as having at last brought literary study to a condition rivaling that of the sciences." [8] But could the critics have been both things at once? Is it likely that beneath the chilly mask of the scientist lurks an aesthete, ripe and exotic in his decadence?

At any rate, one could not easily accuse a solid humanist like I. A. Richards of aestheticism; nor, in my view, the Southern critics, who from the beginning have tended as a group to turn toward moral or social criticism in the manner of T. S. Eliot. Ransom's prose, of course, has always had a certain calculated tone of foppishness, and I suppose that in a time of political and economic turmoil remarks like the one in *The World's Body* that "the object of a proper society is to instruct its members how to transform instinctive experience into aesthetic experience" could seem both glib and irresponsible.[9] And perhaps R. P. Blackmur's more recent adventures in style might suggest that the swollen aestheticism of nineteenth-century decadence has at last come, in his work, to the point of suppuration. Yet the New Critics have been almost heroically prompt, on the whole, in the wish to cure themselves of excess and deviance. T. S. Eliot, sometimes thought of as a founder of New Criticism, urged as long ago as 1935 in his essay, "Religion and Literature," that the critical act is incomplete until the concerns of ethics and religion have also been brought to bear upon the literary work.[10] Tate has also insisted that literary standards, "to be effectively literary, must be more than literary." [11] And Ransom and Blackmur, if in their different ways they have sometimes sounded too much like aesthetes, have written most eloquently—perhaps somewhat penitentially—on the theme of the vital relation of literature to life's deepest moral and intellectual concerns. A major theme of Ransom's has been that art completes man by restoring to him some of what has been taken from his human nature by his brute needs and appetites—the possibility of innocence, of love, even of religious awareness. And Blackmur has urged in "A Critic's Job of Work" that criticism, by virtue of the very nature of literature, is inherently involved "with the establishment and appreciation of human or moral value." [12] The charge of aestheticism, as we shall see presently in still greater detail, was assuredly an ill-founded one, at least so far as the critics' deepest convictions and best intentions were concerned.

But the alternative idea, suggested by some of the critics themselves as well as by certain commentators on them, that the New Criticism represents some sort of classicist or neo-classicist viewpoint is just as faulty. It is true enough, as the textbook discussions claim, that the typical New Critic, deriving much of his baggage of assumption and prejudice from the Hulme-Eliot-Pound sources, consciously opposed some beliefs, tendencies, and artistic manners pertaining to the Romantics. He was even likely to be a classicist, in the sense of conservative and traditionalist, in his political and religious preferences, though this might be more relevant to the American New Critics than to the English. Perhaps he was a classicist, too, in the poetry he chose to praise—at least insofar as he believed that poems should be "art" rather than occasions of the poet's free expression of emotion. But even with all this, when we scrutinize the New Critic's aesthetics, epistemology, and metaphysics, it makes much more sense to describe him not as any sort of classicist but rather as a version of *romantic*. We find, for example, that he speaks freely and frequently of Truth and Knowledge without referring them to observation or logic or clear dogmas; that sometimes he looks upon poetry as a means of getting into contact with "higher" realities; and that he is often fervid in his discourse, rather than "rational." My point is that though the New Critics may have proposed certain classicist-like principles and ideas, they have actually harbored and nourished within their criticism a viewpoint or sensibility that is romantic in kind. And it it this romanticism of viewpoint or sensibility which most truly constitutes, in my view, the "real" identity of the New Criticism as a literary movement, the identity by which it *should* be, whether or not it will be, remembered in literary history.

I think it is no exaggeration to say that the influence of the New Critics has been strong and widespread enough to mark their cause as perhaps the most extraordinarily successful of all consciously waged literary revolutions. But the very size of the success, as we have already seen, makes it, like *Paradise Lost* to Edgar Allen Poe, almost too big to be apprehended clearly and wholly as a unity. When we may now find a lecture by Ransom published under the auspices of the National Council of the Teachers of English,[13] when Cleanth Brooks' name may be seen comfortably appearing in the membership lists of the Modern Language Association, and when *Kenyon* and *Sewanee*, traditionally organs of the New Criticism in the same way that *PMLA* is an organ of "scholarship," can be found printing such historical scholars as Miss Tuve and the gadflyish Professor Bush, we may begin to wonder what, in the dialectics of controversy, the New Criticism really was. Brooks has said that Ransom originally used the term *New Criticism* as a "neutral and modest designation; i.e., the modern criticism, the contemporary criticism." [14] But this doesn't help much, of course, because we have ample evidence that all during the forties there was a squabble about *something*. One thing we can be certain of, thanks principally to the polemic activities of the New Critics: it is no longer possible to believe, as Howard Mumford Jones apparently did in 1934, that the scholar's business is only to be "the historian of literary culture," and that therefore "we should be grateful when the scholar is also a critic, but we should not be surprised when he is not." [15]

The significance of the New Criticism so far as literary history is concerned lies somewhere in the success of its rebellion, in the cause of literature, against unliterary and uncritical academicism. There was a time, say from twenty-five to thirty-five years ago, when most academics, being neither critics nor men of letters but "scholars," had actually allowed a separation to appear between their activities as scholars and the humane values which literature and the arts have been held traditionally to contain or represent or nourish. There followed a time, during the forties principally, when the rebel critics who had attacked "scholarship" and "irrelevant" quests for "facts," were in turn accused of going aestheticist, or of willfully ignoring "facts," or of abandoning man and his social problems; and in more recent years the critics have even lectured themselves on the dangers of critical autotelism. But as Lionel Trilling wrote a few years ago in a review of Professor Douglas Bush's *English Literature in the Earlier Seventeenth Century*, now "scholarship and criticism drink together at whatever classical fountain you choose to name, and we wonder what all the old shooting was about." [16] Out of the conflict has come a period of increased depth and harmony in literary study in which both scholar and critic, whatever their differences, seek to be more whole and humane in their dealings with literature. And I think the large importance of the New Criticism is very securely founded on its responsibility for creating, through its polemic and literary successes, this generally healthier literary situation.

The importance of the New Criticism as a force in recent literary history is, of course, attested to by the fact that so much has been and is being written about it. Toward the end of the forties certain works began to appear that tended to shift the status of the New Criticism from "controversial" to "classic." Stanley Edgar Hyman's *The Armed Vision* (1948), for example, did not limit itself to the New Critics, but there is an indirect tribute to the scope of the New Criticism's successes in the very fact that Hyman's serious and complexly learned book about modern criticism aroused such widespread and energetic interest. A year later two other studies, both monuments to the New Criticism, were published: one was William Elton's "A Glossary of the New Criticism," which sold out when it was first printed by *Poetry* and had to be reprinted to meet the demand; the other was R. W. Stallman's *Critiques and Essays in Criticism*, which was a compendium of important pieces by New Critics and some of their followers and associates, with an appended massive bibliography of modern criticism and two discussions of the New Criticism as a major movement, one by the editor and the other by Cleanth Brooks. John Crowe Ransom's anthology, *The Kenyon Critics*, appeared in 1951, and William Van O'Connor's *An Age of Criticism*, a brief handbook on recent criticism, chiefly New Criticism, appeared in 1952. And I think it would not be unfair to say that W. K. Wimsatt, Jr. and Cleanth Brooks' *Literary Criticism: A Short History* (1957) caps the intention of most of these works by interpreting the whole history of criticism in the West teleologically in terms of the New Criticism as the implicit *telos*.[17]

But in the fifties another kind of commentary on the New Criticism began to be heard, a less partisan, sometimes more intellectual kind that sought to understand and evaluate it more objectively in the light of modern literary and intellectual history at large. In 1950–51 *The American Scholar* published a discussion of the New Criticism in which William Barrett, Kenneth Burke, Robert Gorham Davis, Malcolm Cowley, Allen Tate, and Hiram Haydn were the participants. The discussion attempted to define the nature of the New Criticism as an ideological movement, and the New Critics, taking exception to certain exclusive interpretations of their politics and aesthetics, seemed to see themselves as representing no more and no less than a renewal of the general humanistic tradition. And it is just that interpretation, differently colored and shaded in each case, that supplies the implicit common ground of agreement between such widely divergent appraisals of the New Criticism as C. Hugh Holman's approval in his "The Defense of Art: Criticism Since 1930" (1955) and Karl Shapiro's disapproval in *In Defense of Ignorance* (1960). Two more neutral and detailed studies are John Bradbury's *The*

Fugitives (1958), an intensive evaluation of the creative work of Ransom, Tate, Penn Warren, and certain others in the light of the development of their critical theories and principles, and Louise Cowan's *The Fugitive Group* (1960), an elaborate historical examination, on the basis largely of primary biographical materials, of the early development of the same group's thought and art during the twenties. Among the growing number of recent articles that indirectly or directly concern themselves with the system of "thought" behind the New Criticism—its aesthetic or poetic lore—are those which emphasize the incompleteness, the "monism," as Professor Crane would say, of New Critical theory. They tend to understand and judge it in terms of what they think it excludes from consideration—such as "style" (style as the sensibility or felt personality of the author), or "history" (not as "fact" but as vision), or "reality" (as cause and referent of the work of art).[18] But although these commentators are right about some of the limiting effects of the New Critics upon their many followers, they do not seem to me to represent fairly the adaptability and scope of interest of most of the major New Critics themselves. The fairest and fullest commentator of this kind to date is Murray Krieger in *The New Apologists for Poetry* (1956), which though it is written by a New Critical partisan is thorough both as an analysis and as a critique.

And it is Mr. Krieger's book that provides me with my point of departure. Krieger is systematically concerned with the "structure" of the New Criticism—its philosophy of poetry, its critical organon—, whereas I am concerned with its "texture"—the community of feeling, the perhaps unconscious commitment, the shared *sensibility* of the New Criticism, which Mr. Krieger's findings, like mine, tend to depict as a "romantic" criticism. My discussions will thus be something of a complement to Mr. Krieger's. Where he analyzes ideas, arguments, the integrity of a system, I shall try to illuminate the predilections, biases, spontaneities of response, sometimes almost the "superstitions" that lie behind it, out of range, often, of the ideologue's eye. Although I shall, of course, be dealing all along with "ideas" and their structuring into a literary philosophy, I shall be getting at them most of the time obliquely through examination of the "texture," or the "body," that they find or create for themselves in the language of the critics. I shall be discussing the tropes, the imagery, the patterns of rhetoric which come naturally to the critics as they write, and I shall occasionally be calling attention to the significance of the frequent disjunctions of their language, as the style of a particular sort of sensibility, from the "ideas" it is intended to express.

The justification for this rather "literary" approach to the New Criticism—an approach certainly not usual in discussions of criticism and critical theory—is first, that the New Critics have for the most part written literarily, as essayists rather than as technicians; and second, that their extraordinary success as literary revolutionists is closely related to the *style* of their persuasiveness, the *power* of their conviction. I have already suggested how they made over the scholar-professor into more of a man of letters who had come to recognize that "research" and "scholarship" are preparations for, or subordinate aids to, literary understanding and criticism. As a result, college students today are getting a more literary education from their English departments than was once available. Their tastes are required to be more alive and catholic, they are asked to understand more, and they are taught something of the processes of the critical as well as historical study of literature. And the changes that have come over the professor and student of literature are the measure of the New Criticism's successful creation, or *re*-creation, of the controlling literary sensibility of our time. By encouraging us toward close understanding of texts they have literally taught us how to *read* poetry. And to help us do this they have given us a critical language, or the types of a critical language, by means of which to define and sustain a coherent and meaningful literary culture. Words have power. And the power in the language of the major New Critics is the power of a deeply committed and religiously felt resurgent humanism, whose essentially romantic ethos makes it peculiarly fit to do battle for literature in a world that is both skeptical and yearning, both non-traditional and painfully dehumanized by its own skepticism.

So one of my purposes in the chapters to follow will be to characterize afresh and to redefine, by the methods already described, the New Criticism as a humanistic movement founded on essentially romantic responses and attitudes. I shall be showing that the New Critics as "defenders" of art or "apologists" for poetry have in the long run directed that defense not toward the realization of certain executive formulas for high art or the good society, as is often avowed, but rather toward a religious image of man as the ark of value. In order to accomplish both of these purposes I shall be focusing often upon the apparently unconscious clash within the New Criticism between its overtly proffered traditionalist, or classicist, or anti-romantic principles of art and life, and the inherently romantic sensibility covertly expressed by most of its practitioners, particularly in their more recent work.

chapter 2

The Romanticism of the New Criticism

THE New Criticism's warfare with the academicians began, of course, in the doctrine of "return to the text," which meant simply that scholars ought to be able to read with reasonably detailed understanding the works of literature with which their scholarship deals. The extent of the New Criticism's success in turning the academicians' attention back to the "text" is manifested in the number of younger critics who have made large reputations for themselves through detailed textual studies of authors who were formerly the property of scholars—for example, Robert Heilman on Shakespeare, Arnold Stein on Milton,—and in the fact that academic journals, from *ELH* to *The Explicator*, have become more and more textual and analytical in orientation. In 1956 I. H. Hassan charged that "the Formalist approach" had now degenerated "into an irrelevant and intricate pastime, one that an IBM could probably simulate with equal interest." [1] The truth of the charge lay in the degree to which the numerous followers of the New Criticism were making formalistic "analysis," both in the classroom and in the pages of the academic journals, a critical end in itself. There was danger of a new academicism—the new mechanics of formalist analysis displacing the old mechanics of scholarship, with no access of human or moral value realized in the change. But Hassan's charge is not pertinent to the major New Critics themselves; for as long ago as the forties most of them had begun to shift their emphasis from "the Poem" as a thing-in-itself to Poetry or art as a formal constituent of the human community.

The essays written by most of the important New Critics during the forties and fifties about the "function" of the arts and the relationship of that function to the obligations of the critic are themselves a very important part of the current reappraisal of the New Criticism as a major literary movement. The critics, having fought successfully to focus attention on the poem as a fit object of intellectual study, were now turning to the question, essentially, of the "relevance" of poetry, and of the study of poetry, to the social, moral, and spiritual life of modern man. Matthew Arnold once prophesied an "immense" future for poetry as increasingly the "stay" of humanity in a world where science had destroyed religion and traditional Christian culture. As if attempt-

ing to fulfill Arnold's prophecy, the New Critics from
the beginning treated literature as the dialectical opposite of "science," and tended to ascribe to poetry and
the imagination some of the same powers and values
traditionally held to reside in religion. Though like
Arnold most of the New Critics had been traditionalists
and orthodoxists in their social and religious principles,
the theory of poetry that they were now evolving was
markedly romantic in its humanism, markedly a
"mystique." Its core principle, that poetry provides
"knowledge" of a higher kind than that of reason and
science, seemed virtually to give poetry the status of a
form of metaphysics or revelation. And the language in
which the theory was couched—strongly animistic, full
of echoes of philosophic idealism, heavily weighted with
the esoteric terminology and imagery of theology and
religion—showed that behind the theory there was also
a shared sensibility that was *un*orthodox, implicit with
romantic heresy.

In recent years we have been discovering both indirectly and directly, through such studies as M. H.
Abrams' *The Mirror and the Lamp* and Frank Kermode's
Romantic Image, that the intellectual, spiritual, and artistic debt of our age to the Romantic movement is greater
than we had once realized, perhaps than we had
wished. And since I shall be trying in this chapter to show
how the overtly anti-romantic New Criticism covertly
shares in the general debt of our age to the romanticism

of the last century, it will be appropriate first to say in a little more detail what the term *romantic* can usefully mean in the present context.

Common usage dictates, first of all, that "romantic" attitudes are based in large part on the assumption that the emotions are the fountainhead of man's knowing, meaning, even being. The New Critics themselves have identified the faults of Romantic poetry with emotional self-expression; as Ransom has, for example, in his admittedly "partial" definition of romanticism as "the production of literature consciously devoted to exploiting the feelings." [2] Secondly, the object of the practicing romantic's philosophical interest, the thing known, is not a natural or "rational" object, but something metaphysically grandiose. It is a "mystery," and whether good or evil, a god or a devil, it has about it the aura of taboo: "The nostalgia for the unknown, and the identification of these with the illicit: the desire for the illicit as the available equivalent for salvation"—these are phrases R. P. Blackmur has put in apposition with the word "romanticism." [3] While Blackmur was referring to the decadent side of romanticism and using trivial Emma Bovary as his touchstone, the essentials of this formula also account for the innocent romanticism of Wordsworth and his deeply religious sense in all things of "something far more deeply interfused." Thirdly, the romantic's discursive language, ranging from "dialectic" to incantation, will usually display an impatience with the restrictions and inadequacies of "rational" and "logical" discourse. It will proceed from a faith, however indeterminate, rather than from a skepticism, and it will seek to develop freely, scorning the limitations of ordinary or pragmatic discourse as not merely inappropriate but too confining for its ends.[4]

These, then, are the principal traits I shall be recognizing as traits of *romanticism as a condition of mind or sensibility*. They derive a convincingness and validity by applying not only to the New Critics but to those poets and critics and philosophers, mainly of the nineteenth century, that we know historically as Romantics. The following compilation of claims for poetry and the imagination will suggest how closely the New Critics actually resemble some of these historical romantics, for it is made up about equally of quotations from both groups. And I think it of particular interest that the utterances of the moderns are about as much at home in the contexts of the Romantics as the utterances of the Romantics very obviously are in the contexts of the moderns. Here is the list, arranged in an approximate order of increasing intensity, with the identifications of its inclusions reserved until it has spoken for itself:

1. The notion of the poetic goes along with our notion of intuition, the seized perception in depth.

2. There is something in poetry beyond mere prose-reason. . . .

3. Reason is to the imagination as the instrument to the agent, as the body to the spirit, as the shadow to the substance.

4. Poetry is the completest mode of utterance.

5. The poet, described in ideal perfection, brings the whole soul of man into activity, with the subordination of its faculties to each other according to their relative worth and dignity.

6. If the poem is a real creation, it is a kind of knowledge that we did not possess before. It is not knowledge "about" something else; the poem is the fullness of that knowledge.

7. Now poetry is nothing less than the most perfect speech of man, that in which he comes nearest to be able to utter the truth.

8. Poetry is the supreme use of language, man's chief coordinating instrument, in the service of the most integral purposes of life. . . .

9. The ground-bass of poetic truth is the truth, contextual but real, of man's possible redemption through the fullest imaginative response.

10. Poetry is the breath and finer spirit of all knowledge. . . . Poetry is the first and last of all knowledge. . . .

11. The might [of poetry] is there for the moment when the soul lifts her head.

12. The poet brings forth values with which history is in the pain of labor.

13. [Poetry] is born in the soul at the mysterious sources of being and reveals them, after a fashion, by its proper creative motion. . . . The unconscious from which it proceeds . . . is . . . a more vital and profound unconscious [than the Freudian], the unconscious of the spirit *at its source*—hidden from the inquisitive intelligence in

that density of the soul where all the spiritual faculties have their common origin.

14. Poetry is the *nous poetikos*, that deep habit of mind, deeper than any sea of hope, calmer in its long swell than any mirror of despair, which imitates in forms and images dear to herself the life she has lived, the life she dreads to live, and the life she aspires to live. She looks everywhere about her, for she contains in her own way everything that she sees.

In series these quotations might be mistaken for the responsive reading of a Unitarian service. That they have something of that effect is indicative, I think, of their fundamental nature; they make attributions of large importance to poetry and the imagination; they formulate the attributions in the language of emotion, ranging from piety to virtual ecstasy; they present the formulations epigrammatically or allegorically—that is, in the ambiguous but seemingly definitive forms of oracular statement, of final truth given or intuited. And here are the oracles:

1. R. P. Blackmur.[5]
2. Edward Young in *Conjectures on Original Composition*. Note the astonishingly modern sound, for 1759, of "prose-reason" as the dialectical opposite for "poetry."
3. Shelley in *A Defense of Poetry*.
4. I. A. Richards.[6]
5. Coleridge, *Biographia Literaria*, XIV.
6. Tate.[7]

7. Arnold in the essay on "Wordsworth."
8. Richards.[8]
9. Philip Wheelwright, philosopher and aesthetician closely related to the New Critics, and long-standing contributor to their magazines.[9]
10. Wordsworth in the "observations" preceding the *Lyrical Ballads*.
11. Robert Penn Warren.[10]
12. Eliseo Vivas, aesthetician and follower of the New Criticism.[11]
13. Jacques Maritain, who, though certainly no New Critic, is both a considerable "romantic" and one of the Catholic authorities New Critics are most in the habit of citing.[12]
14. R. P. Blackmur again.[13]

It would not be difficult to develop a different or a longer list of the same sort. But it would serve the same end: to prepare the critics for their characterization as twentieth-century romantics, the sort of romantic that, as I have already suggested, Arnold foresaw in his famous statement on the future of poetry, as quoted from himself at the beginning of the essay on "The Study of Poetry":

The future of poetry is immense, because in poetry, where it is worthy of its high destinies, our race, as time goes on, will find an ever surer stay. There is not a creed which is not shaken, not an accredited dogma which is not shown to be questionable, not a received tradition which does not threaten to dissolve. Our religion has materialized itself in the fact; it has attached its emotion to the fact, and now the fact is failing it. But for poetry the idea is everything; the rest is a world of illusion, of divine illusion. Poetry attaches its emotion to the idea; the idea *is* the fact. The strongest part of our religion today is its unconscious poetry.

And this additional statement needs to be recorded: "Without poetry, our science will appear incomplete; and most of what now passes with us for religion and philosophy will be replaced by poetry."

Here is Arnold's prophecy, in 1888, of what seems to have come at least partially true in this latter day of the New Criticism. It has come true, too, in about the terms in which he meant his prophecy to be understood. Poetry, in itself and standing for the fine arts generally, now has for the critics that central intellectual-spiritual value once held, before science, to reside in religion and philosophy. And the Imagination comes to be seen by the critics as the central integrative faculty of mind whose function seems most of the time to be everything that those of faith and reason, before Science, once were. Sometimes the concept of the Imagination even takes on in the critics' eyes the form of some tragic fable or moral allegory. Robert Heilman's study of King Lear, for example, finds one tragic theme, along with the theme of the collapse of the traditional society, to be that of the tyranny of rationalism over the Imagination.[14] And Robert Penn Warren's essay on *The Rime of the Ancient*

Mariner, which presents the poem in terms of the "One Life" and the "sacramental vision," makes the Imagination virtually synonymous with "salvation" after sins of pride in reason.[15] Both of these critical works are, of course, "interpretations." But they carry with them unmistakable signs of intellectual assent to the discovered themes as "truths," truths proffered in turn by the critics—at least by implication—to modern man as intimations, even revelations, of his own possibilities for salvation.

The critics have not been unaware of Arnold's shadow falling upon them. Some of them, in fact, have been almost as aware of him as they have of Coleridge, though often the awareness has been uneasy. Richards and Ransom are perhaps the two most ready to accept their relationship to Arnold. They sound like him often, and they know it, and sometimes they have been moved to cite him as an authority. *Science and Poetry*, for example, begins with the famous quotation from Arnold and builds upon it as the justification for Richards' psychological poetics and the almost life-or-death importance he attributes to poetry's possible relation to modern life: poetry, he believes, as Arnold seemed to foresee critics might, "is capable of saving us; it is a perfectly possible means of overcoming chaos." [16] *Science and Poetry* represented, of course, the gist of *Principles of Literary Criticism*, which was in turn the theory behind *Practical Criticism*. And though Coleridge became Richards' mas-

ter in theory in the later writings, I think it safe to say
that it is an Arnoldian moral vision of the future of poetry and the spiritual needs of modern man that has motivated Richards' work from the *Principles* to the most
recent essays collected in *Speculative Instruments*.

Ransom has been a little more guarded in announcing
his recognition of Arnold. But it is there nevertheless, if
at a farther remove. In at least one of the essays in *The
World's Body*, for example, Ransom assumes the skepticism of his time and elevates, like Arnold, the aesthetic
and formal values of religion over those of doctrine.[17]
Elsewhere he makes the consequent transference of
value that Arnold made from religion to art, though in
different language: "The miraculism which produces
the humblest conceit is the miraculism which supplies
to religions their substantive content."[18] In the essay on
"Yeats and His Symbols," the transference is recognized
as an actual fact of history.[19] And in at least two other
places Ransom openly acknowledges his concurrence
with Arnold that poetry and religion have "a common
cause"[20] and "refer to the same order of reality"[21]—
although he insists, with Eliot, that Arnold was wrong-
ing religion when he denied its possession of "fact."[22]

R. P. Blackmur bears Arnold out almost everywhere.
Blackmur's thesis in "The Enabling Act of Criticism,"
that we must submit to literature since those inescapable
and fundamental life interests once formed and contained by the whole of Christian culture are now focused

only in literature, has been the foundation of his criticism for the past fifteen to twenty years.[23] In "A Burden
for Critics," an expanded discussion of the same thesis,
Blackmur tries by contempt to avoid association with
Arnold. But he succeeds only in confirming more
strongly the relevance of Arnold by specifically and
pointedly applying to poetry since Yeats and Eliot Arnold's general principle that poetry fills, indeed *must*
fill, the cultural and psychological vacuum left when
Christian culture gave way to the forces of modernity.[24]

Tate's steady antipathy to Arnold, finally, has been a
significant form of recognition. It certainly suggests a
more than usually acute sense of Arnold's contemporary
relevance. And it can be interpreted besides, as it will be
at length in a succeeding chapter, as the expression of
conscience in the twentieth-century romantic—the not-
quite-conscious sense of conflict between his openly
espoused values as a traditionalist and the submerged
but obtaining romantic values asserted and exercised in
the nature of his sensibility.

The interpretation of the New Critics that I propose,
then, is that they are twentieth-century romantics whose
sensibilities *as romantics* overbalance whatever traditionalist viewpoints they may explicitly subscribe to;
that their romanticism has been part of the "romantic
reaction" against science and reason which they themselves have observed and sometimes criticized in the art
and thought of this and the last century; that they have

tended to oppose poetry to science in the manner of the Romantic poets; and that, again like the Romantics,[25] in order to raise that opposition above the level of a merely desperate emotional reaction, they have developed and promoted a supporting theoretical doctrine that poetry is a high form of knowledge. I shall discuss in detail the New Critical mystique of poetry, and its poetry-as-knowledge doctrine, in a later section. But I want to move toward that subject by tracing the evolution of thought of four individual critics who, in their several ways, contributed to the development of that very mystique. Different as the four critics are, the work of each shows, over the years, a shift of critical emphasis from the idea of poetry-as-form to the idea of poetry-as-meaning—from a formal-aesthetical to a moral-spiritual view of the nature and function of art. It is a significant shift, because it shows the critics as typically "modern" men of letters in uncertain quest of value and meaning in a world which looks to them like a chaos or a waste land. They are pilgrims in search of truth. I shall be characterizing them, in the next section, as "pilgrims" in order to underscore the essentially spiritual or religious motif of their seeking; and "truth" is, I suppose, the proper object of poetry conceived of as a high form of knowledge.

T. S. Eliot's return to orthodoxy is, of course, the most famous of such pilgrimages in our time. I have chosen to discuss four critics whose pilgrimages in literary worlds of thought demonstrate special variations of the significance of Eliot's in his more strictly theological one. The first critic, I. A. Richards, in his "conversion" from a scientistic literary theory to a more speculative one based on Coleridge's concepts of "Imagination," represents the typical history of the modern rationalist romanticized, and bears comparison with the reaction of Coleridge and Wordsworth against their own early rationalisms in psychology and politics. The meaning of Richards' pilgrimage is underscored by the example of the second critic, Eliseo Vivas, an aesthetician and follower of the New Critics who abandoned his positivistic school of philosophy for a career as a fierce professional enemy of positivism and a vigorous defender of the arts, metaphysics, and the traditional belief in the "objective" reality of value. Though initially less inclined to any form of reductive rationalism than either Richards or Vivas, R. P. Blackmur, the third figure, exhibits a romantic transformation in the development of his criticism from its early, mainly technical, analysis of texts into its later vividly impressionistic, mystical, and speculative treatment of literature as quasi-religion and virtual revelation. And Allen Tate's pilgrimage, beginning in romantic reaction and moving toward Catholic orthodoxy, represents, finally, the perhaps inevitable choice of the modern man of letters, at least in terms of his dilemma as the critics themselves so often see it, if in his reaction against positivism and the tyranny of reason he is not to fall victim to the opposite demon of romanticism. Conversion to orthodoxy is the logical salvation from the extremes of romanticism implicit in Arnold's prophecy and explicit in the critical practice of R. P. Blackmur.

If modern man wishes to save himself as a human being in an abstractionist society, say all the New Critics, let him turn to literature and the arts. It is this faith which underlies the quests of the four New Critic-pilgrims that I am about to discuss, and which finally brings them all, by their several routes, to that romantic philosophy of literature and criticism—that philosophy, indeed, of the Humanities—that gives the New Criticism its most meaningful identity as a major literary movement. The nature of the salvation promised by the faith and its systematization into a summa of doctrine will become clearer as I proceed. Actually, from this point on the book is all about the meaning of that salvation, and about how certain of the New Critics came, step by difficult step, to their individual visions of it.

PART II

Four Pilgrims

Sometimes I think that life is a dream, and that what I am really doing is not what I do.
ALLEN TATE

chapter 3

I. A. Richards: From Laboratory to Imagination

To MOST observers the publication in 1935 of *Coleridge on Imagination* signaled a very important change in I. A. Richards' thinking as a literary critic. At the time, most other men of letters interpreted it as a shift away from "positivism." But what seems more interesting now is that it was also a shift *toward* a condition of mind that is pretty accurately described by the word "romanticism." It was indeed, as John Crowe Ransom once remarked, a kind of "conversion." [1]

Of course, Richards was never a very good positivist—never a very *pure* one—and much less a scientist, as the standard protests against the pseudo-psychological machineries in the *Principles of Literary Criticism* have demonstrated. He has always been interested in metaphor as a subject of speculative discussion, and he has sometimes tended to forget that his own metaphors were not quite *statements about* events, but rather, in a sense, *imitations of* them. It was perhaps this naturally creative or imaginative bent in Richards that from the beginning prepared the author of the *Principles* for the authorship also of *Coleridge on Imagination* and *The Philosophy of Rhetoric*. But the *Principles* and the earlier general books with C. K. Ogden were the products nevertheless of a consciously analytical motive: to reduce the traditionally impressionistic or religiose language, as he saw it, of philosophy and aesthetics to its simple meanings; to make its content available and pragmatically intersubjective for occasions when people had to use it or talk about it; to, in short, translate it reductively into a workable language for dealing with real problems. And those problems centered around the piquant mysteries of the mind's workings with words themselves.

In surveying the results of Richards' early reductionist motive, one is first struck by the pervasive linguistic skepticism of his early work, his worry about precision in philosophical discourse, his preoccupation with the dangers, in any discursive writing, of heady, emotionally charged expression. "I have comforted myself," he wrote in apology for what he imagined was the dryness of the *Principles*, "with the reflection that there is perhaps something debilitated about a taste for speculation which requires a flavouring of the eternal and the ultimate or even of the literary spices, mystery and profundity." [2] His warnings in the same book against "bogus entities, usually hypostatized words," and his disdain for "Mystic Beings . . . sheltering in verbal thickets," are of course well known.[3] The *Foundations of Aesthetics*, written earlier with Ogden, is a major exemplification of these attitudes, being in substance an extended semantic analysis of several formulations of that very big word Beauty.

But more significant than the verbal skepticism was the early Richards' general skepticism about "theory" in the philosophically speculative sense, and about the craving for lofty and broad generalization that nourishes upon bogus entities and verbal thickets. In the *Principles* he maintained that "no special ethical or metaphysical ideas need be introduced to explain value." [4] In *Science and Poetry* he was impatient with the long-standing speculative contention over the relative epistemological status of science and poetry.[5] And in *Practical Criticism* he tried to discourage quests for a "theory" of poetry that would account definitively for a complex psychological phenomenon, the reader's moment of "assent" to a poem. The place he was willing to allow theory was secondary, dependent, perhaps only rhetorical: "All that arguments or principles can do is to protect us from irrelevancies, red-herrings and disturbing preconceptions." [6]

In the light of all this it was inevitable that whatever literary or critical "theory" the early Richards was to permit himself would be conceived in the image of "science," because science implies an initial skepticism, a dedication to empirical procedures, and a purpose that is finally practical. The science—or near-science, as some prefer—most applicable to studying the experiences arising from art was of course psychology. So in the *Principles* Richards wrote about the value of the arts in terms of their theoretically measurable and practical effect of "organizing" our minds, his theory being that through intelligent experiencing of the arts our minds pass from relative chaos to relative order, from a condition relatively wasteful of their inherent resources to one relatively complete in its realization of them.[7] The way the mind gets ordered, whether or not by art, Richards presented as an essentially mechanical process, which was in accord with the nature of his theory. According to his theory, our thinking, as well as simpler sorts of action, is dependent upon the nature and relative organization of our "interests." "Every interpretation," Richards wrote in *Practical Criticism*, "is motivated by some interest, and the idea that appears is the sign of these interests that are its unseen masters." [8]

It was not long before John Crowe Ransom, reacting as a traditional humanist, reached down his dictionary and in a moment of urbane etymological outrage confronted Richards with the extreme implications of his mechanical interests doctrine: "*Inter-esse,*" he wrote in *The World's Body*, "means to be environed, and interest means . . . to obtain a cognition, to do what Mr. Richards wickedly denies to poetic experience and grants exclusively to sci-

ence: to seek the truth." [9] The details of Richards' theory did in fact deny the New Critics' doctrine that poetry is knowledge. But in effect Richards had already
answered Ransom's protest in the *Principles* by passing
the type of argument it exemplified through the machinery of his psychological reductionism. Because our
minds undergo formation and organization when we
successfully submit them to high art, Richards' analysis
goes, the *feeling* ensues that we have gained illumination,
have come into the possession of new knowledge. Thus
the theory of poetry as knowledge and its sister "revelation doctrines." [10] Such feelings of "revealed significance," he concludes, are not evidence of an access of
real knowledge, but rather only "the conscious accompa-
niment of our successful adjustment to life." [11]

In such passages Richards was trying to make distinc-
tions between actualities and feelings of actuality in order to clear up certain discursive misunderstandings. And
his famous distinction—psychological, it should be
noted, not substantive—between "scientific" and "emotive" uses of language, which asserts that prose, or scientific discourse, is constituted by (factual) statements,
while poetry is constituted by "pseudo-statements," is of
exactly the same order. The attacks on the early Richards—and most of the memorable ones were made by
New Critics—centered upon the inflammatory label
"pseudo-statement." There are unfortunate associations
of disparagement, certainly, in the prefix "pseudo," asso-

ciations that, like the red rag to the bull, so angered the
critics that they were unable then or ever again to see
what Richards had really said. All he had done, really,
was give a name to a psychological distinction that even
his attackers have never, to my knowledge, denied is real.
The intentions of the artist about the way the discourse
of his poem to be taken (and the way the normal reader
in fact takes it) are quite different from the way the discourse of the non-artist is meant to be taken (and is in
fact taken). The "normal" poet does not propose that his
poem be taken as statement, verifiable and capable of being acted upon, nor do we as "normal" readers take it
that way. Richards was doing no more, then, than providing a formal means of designating two distinct psychological relations which may be maintained by an author or a reader toward the language that passes between
them.

In 1931 Richards tried patiently to explain to Middle-
ton Murry, who had piously risen against him, that he intended no "contemptuous nuance" in using the term
"pseudo-statement." It was, he said, "a mere neutral
technicality, to stand for a form of words which looks
like a statement but should not be taken as one." "For
me," he asserted with unmistakable clarity, "*a pseudo-
statement may perfectly well be true;* but, for him, I had
implied that it was equivalent to a false statement" (my
italics).[12] I am not aware that the critics, or Mr. Murry,
ever bothered to understand Richards on this point. And

he seems never to have tried very hard to make them understand. True, Richards has now been forgiven for his
supposed sin against poetry. Though they have never
quite forgotten his early positivist transgressions against
poetry, most of the critics viewed the appearance of
Coleridge on Imagination in 1935 as the document of a
virtual conversion experience—an experience not unlike
Coleridge's own "conversion," as Richards himself has
spoken of it, from Hartley to Kant. Cleanth Brooks expressed his satisfaction, in *The Well Wrought Urn*, that
Richards, having abandoned the hope that poetry could
"save us," now assigned poetry a "more modest place,"
and that he had "reinstated philosophy." [13] Ransom had
tentative reservations about the "conversion" being one
to "idealist philosophy," but with the publication of *The
Philosophy of Rhetoric* a year later he cheered the new
Richards unreservedly for abandoning the "affective"
approach and returning to "objective literature itself"
complete with "the cognitions." [14] And Father Walter
Ong happily found in *How to Read a Page* and the Basic
English version of Plato's *Republic* "the strongest con-
firmation to those who have long believed they discerned in his thought the direct vision necessary to the
metaphysician." [15]

The change in Richards' work as a critic and theorist
of literature is vividly apparent at the level of language.
Beginning with the *Coleridge*, he is increasingly willing
to have his terminology mean more, willing, that is, to

speak more loosely and emotively in areas where it had
been formerly a matter of principle with him to speak,
and have others speak, with restriction and precision.
This means not only that he is less annoyed with other
people's verbal thickets, but that now he seems actually
to set about cultivating a few of his own. The earlier
Richards would surely have objected, for example, to the
later Richards' defense of Coleridge's vitalist view of
"the mind" as preferable to the mechanist view. Coleridge's "conception of the mind as an active, self-form-
ing, self-realizing system," wrote the later Richards, "is
plainly an immense improvement." "As an instrument
for exploring the most intricate and unified modes of
mental activity—those in poetry—its superiority seems
overwhelming." [16] The analytically-minded positivist,
which Richards once was, would very likely protest that
a mysterious conception could not be a very useful or
productive "instrument" for examining, in turn, a mystery. And he would probably "explain" Richards' pref-
erence for the vitalistic instrument—much as the earlier
Richards explained psychologically other people's belief
in poetry as "revelation"—as an *emotionally satisfying*
idea, an idea that encourages and sustains one's sense of
excitement rather than directing scientific attention to
some empirically defined state of affairs "out there." He
would say that Richards' defense of the Coleridgean conception on pragmatic grounds was patently a way of jus-
tifying a belief that was first and foremost more *desir-*

able. He might even grow wry about Richards' own transformation into something of a Mystic Being more interested in mysteries than in solutions to them.

Many of Richards' earlier intentions and principles were, of course, verbally adhered to in the later work. But even the old key words nevertheless have a tendency to change their coloration. *The Philosophy of Rhetoric,* for example, adumbrates a new "science" of language to correspond with how we actually use it, an intention re-iterated in the more recent *Speculative Instruments,* where one essay urges a "United Studies" "at once more scientifically and more humanely conceived." [17] But the "science" of the first quotation now connotes less the laboratory and protocols than it does a classical sort of pursuit that might be designated by a sense somewhere between "inquiry" and "discipline." And in the second quotation there is no question that Richards would place particular emphasis on the "humanely," locating his humane ideal farther away from the scientistic iconography of the *Principles* and closer to the idealistic literary mystique of Coleridge.

A good sample text will be of interest at this point. Here is a well-known passage from *The Philosophy of Rhetoric* on the nature of language:

Words are the meeting points at which regions of experience which can never combine in sensation or intuition, come together. They are the occasion and the means of that growth which is the mind's endless endeavor to order itself.

That is why we have language. It is no mere signalling system. It is the instrument of all our distinctively human development, of everything in which we go beyond the other animals.[18]

The anti-behaviorist tendency to stress the difference rather than the likeness between man and the animals, and the assertion that language is more than a mechanical operation ("signalling system") indicate how far Richards has gone in the direction of abandoning his early reductionist motives and assumptions. The comfortable pairing of "sensation" and "intuition," furthermore, implies some willingness now to regard intuition, or the nonrational, as an avenue of knowing. And the evoked pathos of the ever separated "regions of experience" combines with its context to provide a touch, perhaps, of the "literary flavouring" that Richards had banished from participation in the *Principles* eleven years earlier. It is noteworthy, finally, that in this account of how the mind works with words there is a total absence of the mechanist's jargon of "interests" and "impulses," and that words are now seen to be endowed with a kind of life of their own.

In fact, early in *The Philosophy of Rhetoric*, Richards complains pointedly that psychological theories identifying "thought" with muscular movement are self-refuting; and though he might find them of interest as "hypotheses," they are "too large to have interesting applications." [19] Yet Coleridge's ideas, notorious for their difficulty and ambiguity, are somehow *not* too large. This is because, under the influence of Coleridge, Richards' attitude toward psychology—and thus, for him, toward all types of theoretical inquiry—had undergone anthropomorphosis. In the *Coleridge* he observed that for Coleridge the very possibility of philosophical inquiry is centered in *self*-consciousness, in the contemplation not of the object but of our awareness of the object, which was the essence of Coleridge's notion of the "coincidence of an object with a subject." "The rest of his philosophy," Richards wrote (and I would judge, most of the rest of Richard's own, as an adaptation of Coleridge), "is a verbal machine for exhibiting what the exercise of this postulate or this act of contemplation yielded." [20]

I think such passages as those we have been citing illustrate the essential meaning of Richards' "conversion." All of them implement the dethroning of the scientistic icon, with its attendant statistical and instrumental imageries and its doctrines of precision and objectivity, and the elevation in its place of a modern romantic version of the humanistic icon: Man—sensitive, intuitive, complex, free and creative in his ceaseless quest to realize the fullness and splendor, and perhaps the tragedy, of his own nature. There is the tone almost of contrition in this sentence from a recent essay collected in his volume *Speculative Instruments:* "I did hold, *and still do*, that science is true—i. e. that it says verifiable things—but to protect us from thinking that it is true in other and equally important senses is just what we need Philosophy . . . for." [21] The earlier Richards would respond, of course, by protesting his inability to understand the meaning of such a statement: he would not be able to imagine what other senses of *true* might exist outside the defining principle of at least theoretical verifiability. But with the publication of the *Coleridge* Richards had already taken his idea of "science" far beyond the principle of verifiability: he had anthropomorphized science into "myth," and in keeping with his new taste for increasingly ambitious generalization he had made it one with poetry and myth proper as, like them, a mythic means of encompassing reality and "organizing" our minds.

Here is Richards' conception of myth, as stated in the *Coleridge:* "The saner and greater mythologies are not fancies: they are the utterance of the whole soul of man and, as such, inexhaustible to meditation. . . . They are these hard realities [of life] in projection, their symbolic recognition, co-ordination and acceptance." [22] Richards argues that science and history are also myths in the Coleridgean sense of interpretations or formations or projections of our experience, with their verifiability as an extra and nonessential differentia. Richards sees the obtaining myth of our time as our very awareness of our own disorder, our sense of being cut off from the past, of having lost touch with the great myths themselves. The result, Richards maintains in an enriched echo of Matthew Arnold, is that the role of ordering our minds is forced necessarily upon the poet: "And it is only another aspect of the drift by which knowledge in all its varieties —scientific, moral, religious—has come to seem a vast mythology with its sub-orders divided according to their different pragmatic sanctions, that the poet should thus seem to increase so inordinately in importance." It is Richards' final hope, and he alludes not only to Milton but, significantly I think, to the hopes also of Blake, Wordsworth, and Shelley, that poetry, "freed from a mistaken conception of its limitations and read more discerningly than heretofore, will remake our minds and with them our world." [23]

Cleanth Brooks' impression that in *Coleridge on Imagination* Richards' ambitions for poetry had become more "modest" is not borne out by the book itself. Quite the reverse, in fact, is true. What in all probability moved Brooks to approval was that Richards seemed now to be treating poetry less psychologistically, more humanely. And that the good things—poetry and myth and practical science and philosophy—had now somehow got all stirred up together seems to have muddled Brooks' ability to see that the poet and poetry had nevertheless floated resolutely to the top. The new Richards' comprehensiveness and appetite for speculation have pleased most critics, and that has something to do no doubt with the fact that Richards' romantic "conversion" in the mid-thirties prefigured the mythic, the speculative, the

quasi-theological interests that have come into full
flower in the work of the leading aestheticians and literary theorists of the forties and fifties. Only a few commentators have taken exception—a semanticist here and
a logical positivist there, with hardly a literary man in the
lot. The objections have been of a predictable sort—the
sort voiced by F. R. Leavis in his dissenting opinion on
Coleridge on Imagination when he complained of Richards' "uncritical satisfaction with words" and his failure
to fulfill in practical terms his excited promises of a great
new critical "science" based on Coleridge.[24] These are
the kinds of objections that poets no doubt hear when
their pseudo-statements have been taken as statements.

But I think Richards, about whom so much has been
said by so many, ought to be given the chance here to say
a final word or two for himself. He has been very pa-
tient with his critics, by most of whom he has been pretty
consistently misunderstood. In his latest volume of essays
he writes of the *Principles* that he did not intend in that
book to make a defense of scientism, and he cites from it
an unequivocal passage which clearly opposes the tyranny of the scientific attitude.[25] He says also, and very
rightly, as I believe, that "what influence the book has
had would have been different if more of those who have
discussed it had read it." [26] He reiterates, too, a contention made more than a quarter century ago, in the *Coleridge* (p. xv), that the differences between his earlier and
his later work lie in the language rather than in the

thought. In going over the *Principles*, he writes, he is "more impressed by its anticipations of my later view than by the occurrence of anything to retract. I changed my vocabulary and my metaphors somewhat . . . to present much the same views again." [27]

Well, this is true enough—if we reduce Richards' later writings to their bedrock paraphrases. But if we have learned anything at all from Richards, we are likely to have learned the principle that the natures of vocabularies and metaphors reflect what is going on in the minds that choose and combine them, that changes in language mean changes in the quality and coloration of the thought they embody—changes, that is, in "sensibility." And sensibility is what we have been examining all along. How greatly that sensibility has transformed itself is most evident, perhaps, in the verse Richards has been publishing in periodicals over the past ten years or so, and that he collected in his first volume, *Goodbye Earth and Other Poems* (London, 1958). They tend to be gnomic, cryptic, emergently mystical. One called "Not No," a Coleridgean sort of poem that confronts disbelief in immortality with an intuited sense of mind or imagination as supernatural force, begins with this Delphic prose headnote: "The mind is compared to an empty house animated by the piping gale. Responses to this view and to these responses themselves and to whatever utters itself in this image are included in the comparison." Most of the poems discover, in an almost Emer-

sonian fashion, symbols of spirit in the merest occasions
of matter. One called "Lighting Fires in Snow," for example, makes fire-building analogous to poem-making.
Choice, consciousness, and care tamp down the cold site
and construct the tent of sticks; but then the outside
power, fire, must be let free, independent of the con-
structive rational will, to consume and complete the
whole intention. The poem ends,

> The wise poem knows its father
> And treats him not amiss;
> But language is its mother
> To burn where it would rather
> Choose that and by-pass this
> Only afraid of smother
> Though the thickening snow flakes hiss.

The mystical or revelatory concerns of Richards' verse
center, characteristically, in language—the "magic," the
revelations available in the wonderful workings of
words. One poem called "Perpetuity," which considers
the ambiguity of the river Time as both giver and taker-
away, ends with this prayer in behalf of the imagination
—the spell or incantation of the new Richards as mystical verbalist, who everywhere demonstrates his romantic
faith that words have, in some literal sense, a mysterious
and deathless "life of their own":

> May *may* become
> While *would* would waft
> O let *let* be
> Our sum, our raft, our quay.

Allen Tate has described very perceptively the meaning of the shift in Richards' sensibility from a positivist to a romantic congeries of motives and perceptions, and I can do no better than to end with his words. "Mr. Richards' books," Tate writes in the essay "Literature as Knowledge," "may be seen together as a parable, as a mythical and dramatic projection, of the failure of the modern mind to understand poetry on the assumptions underlying the demi-religion of positivism." [28] There could be no more forceful way of making the point. Unless, perhaps, to observe that this romanticized positivist has in his sixties begun to give us, for the first time in his life, plays and poems—proof of a new access in himself of Imagination, or of Imagination renewed.

chapter 4

Eliseo Vivas: From Nature to Spirit

IN THE pilgrimage of Eliseo Vivas we find represented, in addition to the change in sensibility sketched in the preceding pages on I. A. Richards, an actual change in official philosophic loyalty. Vivas was for some years connected with a modernist semi-positivistic school of philosophy known as the New Naturalism. But he broke with it to become something of a humanist (he now calls himself an "axiological realist") who, in his dual role of philosopher of value and literary critic, performs as a kind of sniper-from-within-the-ranks at all forms of modern philosophic positivism, from the strictly prescribed analytical procedures of the Logical Positivists to the general anti-speculative temper of modern thought as a whole. Vivas opposes the same thing the New Critics oppose—but he gives it a more alarming name, "scientifism." He has become, in fact, if not one of the New Critics at least a follower of them.

Not that Vivas was himself wholly scientifistic in temperament before his philosophic conversion. Even in his positivist days, when he wrote of aesthetic matters with the positivist's habitually restrictive awareness of emotive language, he was capable of feeling that "something new, something unexpected" emerges always in the genuine work of art, "which if it is successful imparts the breathlessness of a miracle." [1] And though Ransom described Vivas in 1941 as having "affiliations [that] are positivist," [2] we can assume from the fact that he served as an Advisory Editor of Ransom's *Kenyon Review* during its earlier years that even then his was a positivism qualified by certain humane loyalties. In those days, furthermore, Vivas was sometimes able to bring his modernist-positivist viewpoint into alignment with his literary interests without feeling either guilt or conflict. In a 1941 essay on D. H. Lawrence, for example, Vivas criticized Lawrence's reaction against the modern world and its scientific orientation as a baffled and childish form of "anti-intellectualism." He concluded the essay with these sentiments, which I suppose could be accurately described as "liberal" in spirit: "The rather obvious truth is that by multiplying the instruments of living science has also created values that former cultures could not even dream of . . . *We could live nobly, and if we do not do*

*so, it is not by resenting science that we will achieve
greater intensity*." [3] (I italicize this last sentence so that
it will come more readily to mind for comparative purposes a little later.)

A modernist liberalism is detectable, too, in the nature
of Vivas' earlier ideas about religion. "I myself . . . believe in God," he wrote in 1942. But when his God turns
out to be "Nature's everlasting energy," we know that
God is only a metaphor for the scientist's moment of
wonder.[4] The essay in which these statements occurred
was a defense of the New Naturalism against an attack
by Philip Wheelwright upon its "materialism." Wheelwright had proclaimed himself to be against positivist reduction and asserted the validity of religion, arguing in
general that religion engages with kinds of reality not
available to the usual empirical investigations. Vivas answered that Wheelwright, who clearly valued both
knowledge and mystery, had allowed himself a little verbal sleight-of-hand in order to claim that "in a loose *but
deeper* sense of the word knowledge, religion involves
mystery as knowledge." Vivas reasonably maintained
that he could not argue where no argument was to be allowed, and took the positivist's normally weary tone
about the language of his more enthusiastic colleague: "I
had always thought it was a philosopher's first duty to
avoid loose talk and eliminate confusion." [5] There is no
mistaking this classic rebuff to the anti-positivist, just
as there was no mistaking in Richards' earlier work the

skepticism, the empiricism, and the verbal wariness of the positivist motive.

But the change that came over Vivas was of much greater amplitude than Richards' gentle and rather gradual modification of sensibility. It was an overthrow, an intense and dramatic revulsion of spirit that issued finally in an almost total reversal of intellectual allegiance. It was in *The Moral Life and the Ethical Life* (1950), as one somewhat ironic commentator has put it, that Vivas "announced to the world his break with the whole naturalistic and humanistic tradition." [6] Vivas described in that work his sense, beginning around 1939 or 1940, of having turned into a philosophic hollow man: "I began to see that the philosophy which until then I had uncritically accepted and which I thought of as the 'new naturalism' could not give an adequate account of certain dimensions of human experience which circumstances suddenly thrust within my purview." [7] In the early forties, he tells us later in Dantean imagery, he was "desperately looking for light to help me out of the dark forest of naturalism in which I suddenly found myself utterly lost." [8] A mainly enthusiastic review of Mrs. Langer's *Philosophy in a New Key* in 1943, which he welcomed because it revived the concept of "significant form" and challenged the pragmatists, naturalists, and positivists, indicates at least the direction from which light was then expected. [9] And in 1948 he took final leave of the old darkness by printing in *The Sewanee Review* a lengthy and vigorous denunciation of the New Naturalism, its "scientism" and "methodolatry." [10]

The general intellectual liberalism that accompanied Vivas' earlier positivist viewpoint was now displaced by reaction. "I have nothing but the deepest contempt for the shallow, Philistine optimism of our world," he writes in the preface to *The Moral Life*, reversing the stand he had taken in the earlier essay on Lawrence.[11] He becomes himself, as he accused Lawrence of becoming, a kind of anti-intellectual. He finds, for example, that Kafka's major dramatic theme is the futile opposition of "intelligence" and stubborn empiricism to transcendent reality, which they will not recognize and accept.[12] He writes of Ivan in *The Brothers Karamazov* that "all he cares about is intelligence. And intelligence by itself is the source of all evil, and ultimately of despair. This is one of the things Dostoievski knew with the same certainty that Ivan knew that he was because he thought." [13] Vivas has learned his lesson, and he seems to see images of its meaning everywhere he looks. Sometimes, as in his admiring essay on that far more suave reactionary, Allen Tate, he expresses anger and frustration even at having to live in this world and this time: "It becomes more and more clear that the positivist mind—whether in its logical positivist variety, or its scientific humanist or its Marxist forms, whether represented by the vacuous rationality of a Carnap or an Ayer, or the vulgar hedonistic secularism of the Deweyans, or the threat-filled dialectic of the commissars—will do its termite work, and there is precious little that any one can do to stop it from destroying our culture." He hears the "muffled despair" in the essays of *The Forlorn Demon*, which suggests to him that Tate "knows that the things he loves are doomed. But Mr. Tate is no man to take the threat lying down." [14] Nor, one concludes from the tone of these passages, is Mr. Vivas.

It is not surprising, in view of the ferocity of his anti-positivist reaction, to find Vivas' earlier reductionist analytical concerns being replaced by a willingness to stretch his vocabulary and enlarge his conceptions in the direction of the metaphysical, the speculative, the semi-mystical. Like Richards, he initiates reconstruction at the level of psychology, recording in the second of the "Two Notes" on the New Naturalism that one reason he had to abandon his naturalistic doctrines was that he had gained a new "insight" that forced him to recognize "the mind's spontaneity": "Once you grasp the importance of the mind's spontaneity you can easily see how naive and simplistic are the efforts of scientists when they try to reduce it to processes of reshuffling with which scientific method can deal." [15] And aesthetics, which he continues to speak of as "an empirical discipline," he now regards as leading on nevertheless to comprehensive "metaphysical" questions.[16] He is even willing to insist, along with his former opponent Wheelwright, upon the existence of real areas of experience and inquiry wholly beyond the self-limited techniques of logic and empirical science. And his conception of philosophy, we can see from the "Two Notes," has become greatly enlarged. If he tended earlier to see the philosopher as something of an intellectual watchdog over language and logic, he sees him now as something of a poet who performs an integrative act of rediscovering the organic oneness underlying the apparently disparate elements of possible human experience: "One of the functions of philosophy is to organize the total content of experience into some sort of viable order of rank. The organization must be accepted not only by the scientist in us but by our whole personality, including whatever vestiges there may be in us of the poet, the saint, the mystic, and the brute animal." [17] Vivas is clearly not unwilling, as he puts it in a footnote to one of his essays, to be counted now among those "who are bold and free from methodolatrous shackles, and who are concerned with the relation of man to culture, and of both to the universe, [who push] out beyond the rim of the positively knowable into areas which fall within the purview of metaphysics and theology." [18]

As one might expect, along with this expansion of philosophical scope has come some considerable emotional intensification, particularly when Vivas confronts his idea of the arts as "constitutive" of our world and as at once "creating" and "discovering" our values. In an essay called "What is a Poem?", for example, Vivas proposes in somewhat melodramatic fashion something like Ransom's notion (via Schopenhauer) of the "be-loved object" as characteristic of the relation between the art object and human consciousness. His rhetoric carries us suddenly into a romantic world of primitivist imagery where the poet in man is awe-struck by the leap of a deer. "But not for long," for the next minute man-as-pragmatist sees food and begins to stalk the animal. Yet man has recognized, during the moment's hesitation, a value other than practical, a feeling other than appeti-tive: "He no longer is mere animal. The woman that would appease his lust has become his mate, the animal he hunts has a beauty that now and then holds his arm long enough to thwart the throw. And he suddenly dis-covers in himself strange needs for intangible things that have nothing to do with his physical survival." [19]

But in certain other contexts Vivas presents these in-tangibles in terms of a different sort of romantic rhetoric, the sentimental jargon of certain belletristic concepts that we are likely to associate with the aesthetic thought of the earlier nineteenth century. Concepts like Shelley's ideal order of Poetry "that makes us the inhabitants of a world to which the familiar world is a chaos" (the *De-fense*); or like Poe's Supernal Beauty for which we weep, since "*through* the poem, or *through* the music, we attain to but brief and indeterminable glimpses" ("The Poetic Principle"). How similar Vivas sounds in this passage from the preface to *Creation and Discovery:* "After the successful aesthetic experience the lingering

memory of the object of art—the more or less clearly
remembered cadenced lines of the poem, or the snatch of
melody and the world of harmony it teasingly suggests,
or the ordered world of color and space of the picture—
these are carried into the mongrel world of actual men,
the world of half-truth and half-dignity." [20] And later in
the same volume he observes, in a somewhat Hamletian
mood, that the "ordered structure" that is an art work
"is ideal, in that its apprehension is rare, and that when
we succeed in grasping it, it brings with it rewards of a
noble kind: peace, serenity, release from the sting of passion and freedom from the indignity of living." [21]

As one might expect, these balloonings of speculative
intention, relaxings of method, and liberations of feeling
result in some philosophic weaknesses—weaknesses, that
is, at least in the eyes of the stricter sort of reasoner that
Vivas himself once was. Sidney Hook has written a full
and technical critique of Vivas' philosophy of value as
formulated in *The Moral Life* that shows the whole system tottering on the verge of logical collapse.[22] And
Henry David Aiken, Vivas' able critic in *Kenyon Review*, has found his aesthetics in *Creation and Discovery*
put "on the stretch" by Vivas' double insistence that the
arts both provide a kind of "pure experience" and also
lead heuristically toward virtual cognitions in the forms
of insight or revelation. Aiken concludes that Vivas' predicament in *Creation and Discovery* is "a kind of para-

digm of the predicament of contemporary aesthetics and critical theory." [23]

But Vivas has in recent years tended to abandon the role of philosopher and aesthetician for the more humanistically limber role of critic and man of letters. And the manner and methods of his later work, even when he reverts to philosophy, tend to be those of the modern critic and man of letters of romantic temperament. *The Moral Life and the Ethical Life* (1950), which is the re-humanized Vivas' testament of value, is a various exhibition of philosophy-by-rhetoric—though a very simple rhetoric: the rhetoric of assumption, irritably passionate assertion, and insistent repetition. This, for example, is how Vivas handles the question of value's "objectivity." An ideal order of values must exist, he says, because the moral controversies people engage in *assume* it. "An order of rank of values independent of their acknowledgment by men in culture must exist, but its determination seems to be, at best, a vague enterprise because the values men know are values-in-culture." [24] Because this ideal order of values has been "assumed," Vivas feels no compulsion to further justify his claim for its existence, even though he sees that evidence for it is something less than overwhelmingly evident. This assumption of values somehow having "existence" apart from an object and a valuer is of course in clear contradiction to the earlier Vivas, who defined value as "any object of any interest;

or more exactly that relational character *in* an object, which arouses an interest in an individual, and which leads him to call the object valuable." [25] He was at that time impatient with seekers after more ultimate descriptions of value: "If as defined," he wrote after applying his common-sense view of value to the matter of aesthetic judgment, "it does not satisfy the hankering for certitude entertained by some men, very well, then it does not." [26] Facts, in other words, are facts.

The later Vivas, however, hankers beyond the mere facts. Taking the position that values are "real" (have "ontic status"), that they are "objective" because they are involved in and we see them "in" objects, Vivas nevertheless feels the need immediately to dislocate his words from their comprehensible content. For the "in," he insists, must not be understood as a spatial term: "Jane's beauty is not in her face like the blue of the Atlantic in a map. . . . Jane's beauty hovers, as it were, above the freshness of the skin, the sparkle of her eyes, the impudent mouth, the dimple of the chin—hovers over the merely physical and, as merely physical, value-free qualities of Jane's face." [27]

This is an example of what I am calling, loosely, philosophy by assertion—that is, by mere verbal stress or shift of stress on top of an assumption that is meant to be elaborated on or provided with an application. Here an assertion is made about the independence of value from Jane's "merely physical, value-free" face. But nothing has been cleared up, much less "proved," by the substitution of one spatial term ("hovers") for another ("in").

Sometimes these insistent declarative maneuvers take place at virtually scholastic levels of abstraction, as, for example, in this utterance about the higher position of "spirit" (an assumed entity) in relation to "psyche" (another assumed entity):

Spirit is highest, and what makes it highest is that, in it and through it only, is the world able to achieve cognizance of its status as creature, to perceive its character as valuable, and through man's efforts to fulfill a destiny which it freely accepts. *This is a metaphysical fact, which I must assume without further proof, accepting as sufficient validation here the intuitive deliverance of my rational consciousness. . . .* [28]

Because they are already assumed at the commencement of discussion, there is no chance to consider questions about the "existence" of "spirit" and "psyche," much less about what the two words mean. Vivas does refer, for additional support, to what he supposes is the concurring "consensus of mankind." [29] But this, of course, is no more than nose-counting—rule by a supposed majority intuition. The earlier Vivas would have been impatient with all this, skeptically insisting, as he once did to Philip Wheelwright, that while knowledge may begin psychologically in intuitions, "they have no hegemony or prerogatives, but must submit themselves to an elaborate procedure of verification of a public nature." [30]

The later Vivas is so deeply committed to the articles of faith that constitute his new philosophy that he is not only willing to reduce himself almost wholly to the declarative method of presenting it, but he expresses an almost moral opposition to semantic and logical analysis as tools of thought. The emotion behind his anti-rationalism is so great that he seems blinded to the most glaring of his own inconsistencies. In one essay in *Creation and Discovery*, for example, he opposes the intrusion of linguistic positivism into the examination of propositions about "the nature of poetry" because, he says, the validation of such statements "depends on facts that are, in principle at least, available to anyone who, endowed with the necessary equipment of sensibility and intelligence, cares to look for himself." [31] In order to exorcise the Logical Positivist, in other words, he invokes the Qualified Reader. Yet in another essay in the same volume he attacks semi-positivist I. A. Richards' appeals to the normative concept of "competent reader" as question-begging.[32] Vivas also frankly, openly, and without embarrassment shifts the properties of his rhetoric when he wants the mood about his subject to go from glad to grim. His doctrine that art "orders" reality is an old one, he admits—a Kantian one refurbished by Cassirer: "But from old truths as from old canvases, the grime of time must occasionally be removed." But a page later the Aristotelians, alas, have on their hands not a precious old canvas but a rotten old corpse: of the concept of art as imitation, he writes, "The present need is not for breathing new life into old corpses long ago buried, but for facing in fresh terms the problems of our age." [33]

While the particular vagaries in Vivas' later work appear to be pretty much unconscious, he is sometimes almost painfully aware of a generalized methodological and linguistic inadequacy. *The Moral Life and the Ethical Life*, for example, contains an almost running apology for the vagueness and indeterminacy of its subject and language. The same is true of some of the literary essays. In "The Object of the Poem," for one, Vivas holds with those who believe a poem "means something," but worries that the phrase is "not much more than an unfortunate muddle which is thickened when we try to explain it by saying that art means itself or that a presentational symbol merely presents itself, and thus does not represent." [34] And of his contention in "What Is a Poem?" that poetry is "constitutive" rather than imitative of reality he remarks, "The reader may observe that I am pushing as far as I can a difference that I seem to have trouble making clear even to myself." [35]

Along with these uneasy doubts and apologies, the later Vivas sometimes displays remnants of the old analytical skepticism about big words and big concepts. Most striking, perhaps, is his reluctance, in spite of his insistence that there are legitimate "areas" of inquiry beyond the range of intellect and the sciences, to go all the way with the critics and metaphysicians and mystics in applying the word "knowledge" to those areas. Even in *The Moral Life* he is inclined to frame the word in skeptical quotation marks, and admits that "outside the exact natural sciences what we call 'knowledge' is a pretty messy product." [36] And in his enthusiastic review of Wheelwright's *The Burning Fountain*, which we may take as the sign of Wheelwright's having had the last and best laugh in their old controversy, Vivas objects to the logic of some of Wheelwright's mythic speculations and the use made of words like "truth" and "knowledge" at the same time that he lauds the book as "an event of major importance for the humanities in our scientistic age." [37]

Whatever they may represent psychologically, these are but token reservations intellectually. For there is no mistaking the completeness of Vivas' conversion, the ferocity of his revulsion against his former liberalism, secularism, and philosophical positivism, the totality of the change that has overtaken his sensibility as a percipient of reality.[38] To speak of Vivas as having completed a "romantic" pilgrimage, furthermore, does scant justice to the particular anguish and bitterness it has involved, and I should expect the term to be taken in this chapter only very approximately as designating the general relationship that exists between the direction of the spiritual quest and the location of its starting point. Vivas' pilgrimage has been a thing darker and incom-

parably more agonizing than Richards' gradual and
organic romanticization. Richards has kept his humor
and his mood of sweet reasonableness, furthermore, and
the change he has undergone has actually fed his natural
liberalism. But Vivas, in contrast, has quite obviously
seen the dark vision and put on the black veil. It is not
accident that Dostoievski is often his point of reference,
for he sees man alternately as sin-ridden beast and as
pathetic fool stumbling after chimeras of happiness that
lead only to unhappiness. "One reason for this," he writes
in *The Moral Life*, "is that the pursuit of happiness is the
pursuit of a mirage, a chase after a travesty of what
spirit really wants—that completion in the Infinite which
alone can slake its thirst." "Anguish is our burden, since
we are placed between non-being and Real Being." [39]

There is often a considerable disparity between the
profundity—even the agony—of his feelings about human and cosmic matters, and the unsophistication of
his expression of them. Often at his intensest moments
the best that the repentant analytical philosopher can
command is the stock manner of Victorian pulpit ora-
tory, the tone of a glum sort of Browning: "The quest
for [moral] certainty . . . defines man's destiny, and
to dissuade him from it is to strip him of his armor
against despair. But it is the quest and not the result of
it that defines his destiny, for certainty is not given to
man to possess." [40] It is not that Vivas is a worse philosopher than the critics he has taken as his new colleagues,

but simply that he does not command that great thing needful—the rich and various expressive, even "artistic," resources of a Blackmur.

Vivas' most recent work, *D. H. Lawrence: The Triumph and Failure of Art* (1960), has the same characteristically Vivasian earmarks: it is irritable and self-centered ("Too long have I lived with Lawrence, feeling always the need to make clear to myself and my students the basic ground for my divided attitude towards him"); it is often badly written—either clumsily or ostentatiously ("He tears the horny cataract of conceptual abstractions from the soul's eyes"); and it is often absurdly literal-minded (as in the heavy-handed "factual" argument with Lawrence's contention in *The Plumed Serpent* that Christianity is foreign to the spiritual needs of the Mexicans).[41] Critically the book is extreme and sometimes blind. But it will be read with interest by two kinds of readers (aside from reviewers); the numerous Lawrenceans, who more than any other species of specialist love to get their teeth into each other, and the much less numerous Vivasians, who for some reason find this most perplexing of contemporary critics and philosophers a fascinating figure. It is exactly the kind of book Lawrence's work most often elicits— the hotly personal response. As his title suggests, Vivas believes his book to be objectively critical—a defining of the borders between the fullness of art of a poet and the abstractionist ravings of a propagandist. Actually it is

the oblique confessional of a terribly upset modern intellectual who knows, like Lawrence, what he hates and
rejects in the modern world, but who unlike Lawrence,
does not know what he believes in and can accept.

D. H. Lawrence: The Triumph and Failure of Art
exhibits an almost classic case of the romantic reaction.
And it seems to tell us, too, that Vivas has not yet become a Christian, certainly not a Catholic. But at least
part of Vivas' "conversion" from Naturalism to a kind
of humanism was assignable, as we have seen, to his
having come into possession of the essential prior vision
basic to Christian orthodoxy in its darker versions. The
last sentence but one of *The Moral Life* affirmed that
final ethical insight frees man and sends him toward "the
source of our freedom and the goal of our salvation.
But this," he concludes, "—which points the way in
which the ethical transcends itself and becomes the religious—is a subject for another essay." [42] I have not
found that this essay has yet been written. But when and
if it is written, it may well reveal Vivas' pilgrimage—like
that of Allen Tate, one of the contemporaries he seems
most to admire [43]—as having brought him finally to the
portals of the Church.

chapter 5

R. P. Blackmur: From Criticism to Mysticism

ONE cannot always be sure what it is fair and honorable to hold R. P. Blackmur accountable for having said. He respects no terminology, he eschews intelligible definition, and objectivity in the ordinary sense is a procedural ideal essentially foreign to his critical performance. He is, in fact, all "sensibility,"—by his own admission "an old Jacobean" in the senses of both admiration and likeness of mind.[1] Blackmur's affinity for James's sort of intelligence and its expression in an elaborately implicative and self-qualifying style was avowed many years ago in the introduction to his collection of James's prefaces. He then justified James's style on the grounds that James "enjoyed an excess of intelligence" which required his style to grow elaborate "in the degree that he rendered shades and refinements of meaning and feeling not usually rendered at all."[2]

The reader who grasped James's artistic achievement and his inevitable pride in it would feel, Blackmur imagined, "the enthusiasm of understanding and the proud possibility of emulation." [3]

Blackmur's own enthusiasm has always been evident, and many of his commentators have believed the celebrated Blackmur style was an importation of his special artistic emulation into the realm of criticism. Most of the judgments of it have been negative. Howard Mumford Jones once contrasted Blackmur—oddly—with Carl Sandburg, who, he said, was "accessible to anyone who can read"; [4] Stanley Hyman has complained that Blackmur imitates James's weaknesses—the "mincing, gingerbread aspects" of his style; [5] some have seen the style as a façade concealing something unfortunate, which Kazin suspected was "a violent narrowness of spirit," [6] and Ransom a general philosophic uncertainty. [7] And because it is supposed to be unusual to find in modern criticism—which we have come to think of as a mainly impersonal and perhaps technical hard labor—a style so unabashedly elaborate and "poetic," it is style that marks Blackmur's individuality.

So it is with the style that one naturally begins in talking about his work. Style is the data of a writer's sensibility; and though there is a notable identity of style throughout Blackmur's work, the changes observable in it over the years direct one's attention toward very interesting changes in the quality of mind and

sensibility that the style expresses and clothes. Blackmur's early essays—those published in the thirties—were
no doubt properly thought of as "Jamesian," or more
Jamesian than the norm, in manner. They were "sensitive" rather than journalistic or academic or ploddingly
methodological, they tended toward a certain prolixity,
and their sentences were reluctant to come to rest without considerable internal self-qualification. But even so,
they were not so "difficult" that they were unintelligible
to most other critical and academic minds. Moreover,
they kept the work always in sight, pursuing in good
New Critical fashion the tasks of analysis and evaluation
that constitute what we normally mean by criticism.
Blackmur saw himself in those years as a technical
critic,[8] but wished "technique" to mean not merely the
"language" of a poem, but all the possibilities for its
illumination, from structure to tropes, even to sources
and influences.[9] And so, Blackmur was in those years un-
dertaking the classic tasks of criticism, New or otherwise, and whatever the Jamesian tendencies of his critical
style, they did not overwhelm those tasks or signal their
subsumption under noncritical or other than critical
ends.

But after 1940 the style turned more and more from the
merely refined, complex, and sensitive toward the tur-
gidly, exotically, almost luridly romantic as the motives
behind the style began to reach beyond the limits of
literary criticism toward something like philosophy,

perhaps toward prophecy. A shift of vision as radical, say, as that required to turn from *Daisy Miller* to *Death in Venice* was taking place in Blackmur's sensibility, a shift toward feelings and perceptions so intense, so dark, so basically *un*civilized, that James would have been baffled and embarrassed before them. Perhaps it was Blackmur's dedicated performance as a practical critic in earlier essays like those on Cummings, Pound, and Marianne Moore that made most of his commentators keep on speaking of him in the same old way long after he had become something rather different. They began to find him harder going, but they seemed generally unaware of the substantive changes taking place. And although they were not always able to follow him now, it was as if this very thickening of difficulties, these proliferant colorings and tonalities of a discourse they were less and less sure they understood, was in itself sufficient reassurance that increasingly delicate and thorough examinations of the old sort were going on somewhere in the essays all the same.

The odd ring of irrelevance in some of the more recent remarks on Blackmur suggests that comprehension of his work, perhaps even the reading of it, may have been dropping off in pretty direct proportion to the continuing ascent of his reputation. Malcolm Cowley, for example, identified Blackmur in *The Literary Situation* in so vague a way that it might have been anyone: "Richard Blackmur has a special feeling for patterns of language, one that casts a new light on any poem he studies." [10] A few years ago Professor Hugh Holman, in a capsule-dose-for-busy-scholars survey of American criticism, summed up Blackmur, apparently on the basis of a rather poorly digested reading of Hyman, in this antithesis: "Analysis is his forte; at synthesis he is not always successful. . . ." [11] And it is strange to find Ransom, who published Blackmur with regularity in the pages of *Kenyon*, still writing of him in a 1953 review of *Language as Gesture* as a "technical" critic, as if that epithet could be applied with equal point to the whole range of his work, from the early dissection of Cummings' poetic language to the late and wholly dissimilar trance-like ruminations on Eliot's "Four Quartets." [12] It was perhaps still stranger, and most disappointing, to have Murray Krieger exclude Blackmur from *The New Apologists for Poetry* on the doubtful ground that Blackmur "concentrates very largely on practical criticism." [13]

Such inadequate conceptions of Blackmur's work—ranging from Cowley's dimness to Krieger's near wrongness—need correction. Blackmur is, after all, a major figure by almost universal assent. And there have been about twenty years now in which to observe the relative shift of his interests, expressed in the increasing stylistic splendor, from technical or analytical criticism of texts toward "theory" and "synthesis" in the largest senses. A few admirers, Stanley Edgar Hyman and

R. W. B. Lewis, for example, have fought through the jungles of Blackmur's later style to see clearly what he was about. But the best brief characterizations of the change that I know have come from somewhat hostile critics. In a 1940 review of *The Expense of Greatness* in *The New Republic* Harry Levin spoke of Blackmur's "soliloquies," and observed that with "less emphasis on craft," Blackmur's "poet's eye rolls farther and farther away from the object." [14] Irving Howe, writing several years later in *Partisan Review* caught the direction of the eye's rolling and the intense mood behind its glance when he noted that Blackmur's shift of interest from texts to "the general crisis of culture" was accompanied by, to quote his handsomely Blackmuresque phrase, "gestures of possessed strain and preparation for prophecy." [15] So the change in Blackmur's style from the relatively functional to the relatively elaborate and personal was paralleled by a change of thematic interest from the critical to the philosophical, from the empirical and executive to the speculative and inspired—a shift, to say it pointedly, toward the romantic end of the spectrum of sensibility.

This modification of style, of subject, of sensibility, is strikingly evidenced by changes in Blackmur's use of certain general terms of criticism—*poetry*, *imagination*, *knowledge*, for instance, and the words denoting the mind's "faculties"—changes in the contexts that shape and condition the uses and defining characteristics of those terms. When Blackmur was primarily a practical critic, though he was even then capable of special enthusiasms for the subconscious and related mysteries, his views of poetry and the imagination had at least common-sense and "rational" leanings. The word "rational," in fact, and related words like "intellect" and "intelligence," often appeared in obviously harmonious, sometimes even proprietary, relationship to the words "poetry" and "imagination." [16] In 1935, for example, he included in an enthusiastic review of *Coleridge on Imagination* assurances to his readers that the Imagination to which Richards had been converted was "above all rational." [17] By rational Blackmur seems then to have meant, to put it most simply, formed by a philosophy, expressive of an ordered mind, rather than itself romantically free and insubordinate. "D. H. Lawrence and Expressive Form" (1935) provided an indirect illustration of his notion of "rational imagination": Lawrence, as a poet in the wasteland, was pure romantic ego possessed by "the demon of enthusiastic inspiration," while Eliot was the poet of what was apparently rational imagination, imagination not free but formed—in his particular case by Christian orthodoxy.[18]

In those days Blackmur consistently opposed poetic anti-intellectualism, whether in the form of doctrines of "pure" poetry, or of poetry as "inspired." He disvalued the poetry of Cummings and "the anti-culture group" because the theory behind it, representing "a sentimental denial of the intelligence," issued in a poetry that pursued "the actual in terms of the immediate as the immediate is given, without overt criticism, to the ego," a poetry in short of "unintelligibility." [19] And in the essay on Emily Dickinson he expressed his impatience with easy beliefs about "poetic mysticism," in connection particularly with Emily's poetry, since their "chief effect is to provide a matchless substitute for the discipline of attention in incapable minds." [20] As these samples indicate, Blackmur was naturally inclined in the early work to encourage, by both example and precept, fairly tough-minded views of language and meaning. Here is a passage from the Cummings essay that I regard as a kind of touchstone of that early tough-mindedness:

True meaning (which is here to say knowledge) can only exist where some contact, however remote, is preserved between the language, forms, or symbols in which it is given and something concrete, individual, or sensual which inspired it; and the degree in which the meaning is seized will depend on the degree in which the particular concreteness is realized. [21]

While this is not a spectacularly precise utterance about language, it expresses sentiments with which one can hardly imagine the later Blackmur being satisfied; for it amounts to something very like a "reductionist," or common-sense, description of how language "means." It is a statement, essentially, of a "correspondence" theory of meaning, it is most certainly empirical in spirit, and it is applied with surprising hard-headedness to language generally—including poetic language, which the New Criticism has usually sought to distinguish as a different "kind" of language from prose.

In the essays of the forties Blackmur's ideas about language and poetry and the mind undergo considerable change, if we may judge from the changes in his use of the key vocabulary in which such ideas are formulated and discussed. To begin with, we often find him explicitly downgrading intellect, and either reversing the normative force of the reason-words or else stretching their application far beyond their usual meaning in order to designate any and all of the mysterious powers of mind that he can imagine. Hyman has observed that in the later essays, as "imagination" and "symbolic imagination" begin to appear more often, " 'intellect' is reduced to a minor role." [22] I think this may be too mild a statement. For in the 1941 essay on "Humanism and Symbolic Imagination," Blackmur's contribution to the controversy between the man of letters and the New Humanism, intellect in the guise of Irving Babbitt is brought to its knees and made virtually to repent its pride and its depredations—the "ravenings of the intellect," as Blackmur puts it.[23] A year later, in an essay on Yeats, Blackmur indulges himself in a little incidental romantic primitivism over the sort of poetry that gets made preconsciously. He says of Yeats' "The Apparitions" that it deals with a kind of experience best understood by the "unlearned," for the "unlearned, who should ideally be, in Yeats' phrase . . . , as ignorant as the dawn, have their own skills of understanding immediately available." [24] This is the sort of understanding available say, to Crazy Jane and Wordsworth's Lucy, but barred to Professor Babbitt. To say the least, such a view is a rather surprising turnabout from Blackmur's earlier suspicions of theories of "mystical" poetry, and it makes room for a *kind* of anti-intellectualism, at least, if not precisely D. H. Lawrence's kind. Perhaps it makes room for the special anti-intellectualism of the modern intellectual-as-romantic—Blackmur's own kind of anti-intellectualism, the kind that makes him quote with an ambiguous and perhaps desperate assent Maritain's "Art bitten by poetry longs to be freed from Reason," [25] and that enables him to have understood so chillingly and brilliantly the evolution—through James, Joyce, Gide, Mann—of the myth and techniques of the artist as modern hero.

The downgrading of intellect extends also to the reason-words—though there is some zigzaggery here that makes inflexible generalization difficult. Our old friend "rational imagination," first of all, suffers denigration in the Babbitt essay along with intellect, for it is spoken of now as "*merely* rational imagination" (my italics). Rational imagination is what Babbitt possesses, and its limitations keep it from knowing what "symbolic imagination" knows—"the knowledge we have above and below the level of mind." [26] By 1948, however, rational imagination appears to have risen again near its former eminence, for in "A Burden for Critics" it is made to stand for the full judgmental responsibility of the critic. But the reason for its rise seems to be that "rational" is allowed now to mean very much more than it meant in the earlier criticism or the Babbitt essay: "What I want to evangelize in the arts," Blackmur writes, "is rational intent, rational statement, and rational technique; and I want to do it through technical judgment, clarifying judgment, and the judgment of discovery, which together I call rational judgment." [27]

In "Between the Numen and the Moha," published in 1954, there is nothing good and profound that "reason" does not mean. It seems to designate there, at the very least, the fundamental principle governing all the mind's activities from the practical to the creative to the visionary: "Reason is . . . the whole mind, the residual form of all we have been, and the conceiving matrix of all that we may become. . . . A servant, the housekeeper who keeps things going by criticism, by philosophy, by art." Though the housekeeper trope is a little puzzling (the essay, involving a good deal of exposition by allegory, is a veritable thicket of wild metaphoric growth), reason's omnipotence as master, it seems, of both philosophy and arts suggests that it has about the force that "soul" has in theological discussion. Yet later on in the essay, reason, though still august, is seen in equal and cheerful competition with art; it is now this very *competition*, in fact, that seems suddenly to be regarded as the fountainhead of "mind": "It is art, by ravishing reason's judgment, that reminds reason of its role. Art keeps reason on its toes, makes it jump and shift its ground, and jump again; for both have the same arena of action. . . ." [28] Here reason, once a constituent of art, even its instructor and controller, appears to have been declared separate again.

"The Language of Silence," an essay on the supra-rational origins and ends of poetic language published in 1955, carries the play with reason still further. At some points we are surprised to find reason-words denoting matters of only secondary importance—in Blackmur's distinction, for example, between the "language of silence," by which he means (I think) language pre-scribed and understood by processes of mystical or in-tuitive knowing, and the lesser "rational" and lyric lan-guages.[29] Yet at other times—when, in a borrowing from Pascal, he speaks of "the reasons of the heart—not the vagaries, but the reasons, of which the mere head knows nothing" [30]—reason-words appear to be denoting mat-ters of the first magnitude. The essay as a whole suggests that the entire work of the poet is governed by something called "reason." Coleridge said something like this. But even he might have been alarmed at the kind of stretch-ing the word undergoes in Blackmur's discussion. For Blackmur, relying once again on Pascal, allows it to apply to everything that goes into a poem, from the relatively mechanical (meter and rhythm) to the relatively magical (feeling and intuition): "Meter is one of the reasons governing poetry; rhythm is another; and there is a third which . . . we call the reasons of the heart of which the reasons of the head know nothing, only in the end we manage the public affairs of the heart's reasons with those of the head, especially in poetry and the verbal medium of thought." [31]

There can be no question about the consistently lowly position, in Blackmur's later work, of "mere head." But "reason"—or at least the application of the term—has no position fixed by definition, and moves athletically up or down the scale of value from mereness to ultimacy, from the common-sense to the magical and the mysterious, in accordance with Blackmur's shifting feelings and rhetorical needs. Lately, of course, the reason-words are happiest to locate themselves as often as they can at the top. But there is no need to flail Blackmur's later utterances with questions in the language of the reasons of the head. Better to submit for the moment, as he would say, to their "rhythm for the language of the reasons of the heart." [32] For when we do we shall know what it is we are here supposed to know: that since the end of the thirties Blackmur has been in pursuit of semantic, emotional, and speculative adventures so wild and so free that we have some considerable justification for characterizing them as romantic.

Stanley Hyman, writing in 1948, observed that after *The Expense of Greatness* (1941) there were signs of a new departure in Blackmur's critical interests: the appearance of "general literary discussions developing themes untouched or largely unstressed in his work before." He named five such essays, and then eight others that were similar to the "earlier pieces on texts." [33] There were most certainly more essays of a general sort in the forties, but the change of interest they represent extends also to those that deal with texts. In the essay on *Ulysses*, for example,—one of the eight analytical essays named by Hyman—Blackmur makes his analysis finally into a consideration of the general alienation of our time from the traditions and institutions of the past, and of the particular alienation of the artist.[34] Like the general essays, it is in the end a discussion of the "modern predicament," concerning itself particularly with the role of the artist and his art as suffering from and ministering to that predicament. The other essays mentioned by Hyman are similarly more than "technical" criticism. They too are general examinations, in terms of particular works, of the special relations of literature to modern life—to, as Irving Howe put it, "the general crisis of culture."

I think Hyman's suggesting a turning point at about 1941 is right enough, though Harry Levin had seen it coming even in the essays of the thirties. I can find no precise juncture, nor do I know of any clear document of romantic "conversion," like Richards' *Coleridge on*

Imagination. But the new trend becomes clear, at least, after *The Expense of Greatness* (1941). What Blackmur's own consciousness of the change amounted to is perhaps best expressed a few years later in the two essays "A Burden for Critics" (1948) and "The Lion and the Honeycomb" (1950). In the former Blackmur urges that the "burden" of modern criticism is "to make bridges between the society and the arts: to prepare the audience for its art and to prepare the arts for their artists." [35] And in the latter he admits for the New Criticism generally that its development of "habitual skills of the analysis of verbal texts" resulted in an undesirable critical insularity—an objection, he writes, that "may with point be applied to myself." [36] Here is something a little like self-recognition, confession, repentance. The critic as technical analyst wants to become the critic as therapeutic humanist, who dedicates himself to revitalizing in both the theory and practice of criticism the moral imperative to relate literature as an art to the intellectual-spiritual problems and needs of man in our time. But the traditional flavor of this imperative somewhat misrepresents, as what has already been said here should suggest, Blackmur's peculiarly romantic fashion of heeding it. For he views the relevance of literature to life not as moral philosopher but as seer. He is less interested in illuminating and strengthening that relevance through the elucidative and pedagogical instruments of the critic than by means of the incantatory and evocative powers of the poet-priest. Blackmur's later essays in general, as Ransom has remarked of the Mann essay, are "transcendental talk," "apostolic and unashamed" [37] in their expression of the modern agony through a quasi-religious commitment to art as the mode of virtual salvation.

Though Blackmur recognizes that orthodoxy may supply needed forms for the mind and imagination of the individual artist, he does not take seriously the notion that the modern world might be reorganized and refreshed by a "return" to orthodoxy and traditional Christian culture. He wrote in an early essay on Eliot (he would not, of course, state his declaration so squarely today) that "a Christian state, a Christian education, a Christian philosophy, are as outmoded as the Christian astronomy which accompanied them when they flourished." [38] Yet Blackmur believes, as Arnold believed, that the mysteries nevertheless obtain—at least as long as we remain human—and that the persisting human sense of them requires avenues of reaching out to them and means of engaging with them, avenues and means once provided by institutions like the Church.

Impulse and silence contain the seeds of gesture and language: this is the relationship of need and cause as "feeling" (to combine a pair of terms from Mrs. Suzanne Langer with a pair from Blackmur) to gesture and language as "form." But the danger is that with the death of the old forms and faiths, the feelings that they contained might disperse and eventually dry up. The purposes of Blackmur's later criticism have centered in an effort to keep that from happening. Blackmur has tried to recreate in his own way Arnold's vision of the "future of poetry," first by encouraging against the current of modern pragmatization and secularization a passion and a reverence for sensed mysteries; and second by discovering works of literature, whether for audience or artist, as experiences which put that passion and reverence into formal relation with the sense of the mysteries, with this discovered relation perhaps finally to be considered a kind of "knowledge." It was something as ambitious and esoteric as this that Blackmur had in mind when in "The Lion and the Honeycomb" he wrote, with a rather irrelevant metaphoric humility for one who is nothing if not virtuoso, that the critic as "go-between" ought to disappear "when the couple are gotten together." [39]

Blackmur's first task, to cultivate the mysteries, is very materially aided by his style. Rhythmic incantation, allegorical indirection, the mystical rhetoric of pun and paradox—these are the sorts of techniques creating in his criticism its distinctive aura of priestly and prophetic power. In "Between the Numen and the Moha," an essay on the purview and function of literature, by geometrizing abstract relationships and allegorizing concepts, by incantation, ritual, drama, he freshly presents in a bizarre sort of prose-poetry an ancient and familiar antithesis. Blackmur goes East for the terms of his antithesis, which is to be the basis of a theory of literature; and soon the classic Ideal and real (in the lower case sense), or their psychological translation into something like "aspiration" and "performance," have become the mysterious Numen ("that power within us, greater than and other than ourselves, that moves us, sometimes carrying us away, in the end moving us forward unless we drop out, always overwhelming us") and Moha ("the uncontrollable behavior which tends to absorb and defile both the chill and the fire of spirit").[40] A pair of familiar old abstractions are thus freshened and transformed into immediately felt mysteries—forces stirringly sensed as in huge interminable struggle just beyond consciousness.

I have said that even the early Blackmur was susceptible to the lure of mysteries. In "A Critic's Job of Work" (1935) he evoked the pathos of the critic stumbling across the mind's plain after mysteries. The critic's approaches were provisional and his mind unredeemably skeptical. But the point was, nevertheless, to "scrutinize and scrutinize," and to "stop short only when you have, with all the facts you can muster, indicated, surrounded, detached, *somehow found the way demonstrably to get at, in pretty conscious terms which others may use, the substance of your chosen case*." [41] Such a passage is another measure of the change in Blackmur's later work; for his earlier intention was not finally to charm man into the unspeakable aura of the mysteries, but rather to convert, translate, reduce the mysteries, so far as he could, to practically speakable terms. Even when the later Blackmur suspends direct evocation of the mysteries in order to "talk about" them, he sounds, at his very mildest, like the enthusiastic metaphysician manipulating the big philosophical words through gorgeous ballets of dialectical opposition, combination, and fruition—with the blush of the romantic pathos showing, usually, on whatever pattern or principle finally emerges. We might imagine we were reading the Schlegels in this passage from a 1951 essay on Eliot:

It is eminently natural that, since reality is a mystery, man's institutions, and especially those institutions which are poems, as they cluster about that mystery, must again and again be made to feel the pressure of the real into the actual, lest the institutions lose their grasp of ideal aspiration and become mere formulae. We only *know* the real by what happens to it and to us; which is a true paradox. Man dwells in the actual, between the real and the real.[42]

The trope here of poems as "institutions" brings us conveniently to Blackmur's second major critical task—the facilitation, through analysis of texts and elaboration of theory, of poetry's performance of functions once proper to institutions that are now defunct or obsolescent. To put it most simply and generally, institutions—and this means broadly customs, myths, religions, the structures of whole cultures—"coped" with the mysteries. With the passing of institutions, art becomes the principal way of coping with the mysteries thanks, as Blackmur put it of James's "added dimension" of theme in *The Sacred Fount,* to "the *prehensility* of the imagination itself in the face of mystery." [43] So literature exhibits or presents essential truths about ourselves and our world, truths which, without art and the imagination, would remain otherwise bifurcated into unrealized abstraction or unconceived experience. Blackmur tries to say how this comes about in this long and urgent rumination on symbolic imagination from "A Burden for Critics" (deletions are largely of repetitive or bibliographic material):

By symbolic techniques I mean what happens in the arts— *what gets into the arts*—that makes them relatively inexhaustible so long as they are understood . . . , what happens in the arts by means of fresh annunciations of residual or traditional forces . . . , those forces that operate in the arts which are greater than ourselves . . . , invokable forces, or raw forces, the force of reality, whatever reality may be, pressing into and transforming our actual experience. It is what bears us and what we cannot bear except through the intervention of one of the great modes of the mind, religion, philosophy, or art, which, giving us the illusion of distance and control, makes *them,* too, seem forces greater than ourselves. . . . It is the force of reality pressing into the actuality of symbolic form. Its technique is the technique of so concentrating or combining the known techniques as to discover or release that force. It is for this purpose and in this way that the executive, conceptual, and symbolic techniques go rationally together: the logic, the rhetoric, and the poetic; they make together the rationale of that enterprise in the discovery of life which is art.[44]

Or, as Blackmur puts it in "Between the Numen and the Moha," literature *exercises* "morals," actualizes them with substance and life. Once they are brought into literature, "the force of behavior refreshes them. . . . In literature morals are compelled to respond to the turbulence of actual life." [45]

The essay on *Anna Karenina* provides a good illustration of how in the later so-called "technical" essays these theoretical ideas are pursued in terms of specific works. Blackmur's subtitle tells us that *Anna Karenina* is an example of "the dialectic of incarnation" in art. The novel incarnates a force which expresses itself in real life in the struggles of men and society to achieve "rebirth, the change of heart, or even the fresh start." These are "partial incarnations" of "that force greater than ourselves, outside ourselves, and working on ourselves, which whether we call it God or Nature is the force of life, what is shaped or misshaped, construed or misconstrued, in the process of living." [46] In the finished novel, however, the force is fully and variously incarnated in the possibilities realized by the various characters. In the past, institutions, in a broad sense, provided the incarnations. But when the institutions became moribund, the novel, as a major art form, had to take over this function. Because there were no longer recognized institutional forms available, the novel's manner of incarnating had to be "dialectical;" it had to begin at the unformed beginning—with raw life, so to speak—and *find out* anew where the momentum of the force leads. As Blackmur puts it, the novel's task is to "create out of manners and action motive, and out of the conflict of the created motive with the momentum to find the significance: an image of the theoretic form of the soul." [47] Blackmur's ensuing analysis of *Anna Karenina* demonstrates the theory by delineating in some detail one such image by Tolstoi.

Blackmur's "apostolic" and "transcendental" interests show themselves in all of his more recent essays, no matter how "technical"—even "textual"—they may be. He is usually, though not always, the literary critic; but he never fails, even when he acts as critic, to assume also the roles of priest to the mysteries and speculative philosopher of literature in its relations to modern life. The controlling idea that emerges from every essay is that literature is of supreme *human* importance—importance of such magnitude, in fact, that Arnold's vision of the immense future of poetry, minus its no doubt hoped-for ballast of middle-class respectability, has been realized most fully in Blackmur's work. For Blackmur's later essays are the closest thing we have to a consciously acknowledged mystique of poetry. Stanley Hyman, who some years ago viewed Blackmur's skepticism and relativism as a sign of profound intellectual "humility," saw at the same time new manifestations ("almost a secular religion of art," "a new attitude, almost mystic, toward art") [48] that later grew into a full mystique. He preferred, however, to stress the intellectual humility—which was not humility at all, of course, but an early form of mystery-mongering. From the perspective of several years later, we can see that humility is not quite the word with which to describe the self-appointed custodian of Mysteries. For as R. W. B. Lewis wrote a few years ago in *Kenyon Review*, Blackmur is "the critic as prophet, announcing to the ungodly the communication of men with ultimate reality." [49]

We might suspect even a certain pride in one who is in love with mystery, with the moving notion that man is, perhaps tragically, condemned always to provisional, even doubtful knowledges. I think Blackmur would be the first to resist the lifting of the veil—the tragic-making veil—from "reality." For mystery *is* his reality. I cannot quite believe, as R. W. B. Lewis believes, that "Mr. Blackmur's journey is a quest for final cause;" [50] much less that the final cause will turn out, after the wayside temptations, to be defined by Christian orthodoxy. Any sort of final cause, it would seem, would be too final, too solid and definitive and static, for Blackmur to accept without disappointment. But he is not likely to run into one anyway because his pilgrimage has, in a sense, been downward rather than upward all along. He has been probing the preconscious and the subconscious, catching hold fleetingly of what is there by prehensile imaginative grasp, gazing up into the "chthonic under-side of things which the topside only keeps down," [51] flirting with Spiritus Mundi. Perhaps he more than con-vert Allen Tate is Poe's spiritual cousin. In an earlier century he might in fact have written "Eureka," the prose poem of the enraptured solipsist. He is the opposite brother of Shelley, whose own romanticism implied his possibility, perhaps his inevitability. For he is intellectu-ally the anti-Promethean who melts reason into feeling, knowledge into mystery, intellect into sensibility, light into darkness. The extraordinary thing is that practically from the beginning—the earlier pieces on Adams and T. E. Lawrence, for example—he has been engaged, like Tate, in a virtual critique of his own sort of ro-manticism, its elaborate decadence, its creativeness, its necessity in our time. The difference from Tate is, I think, that he wholly and consciously accepts it on its own terms.

Irving Howe once asked about Blackmur's role of prophet of "anti-dogmatist insight," "May not the in-volutions of [his] language be a gesture declaring the intolerable problem of thought—the style, that is, doing the work it cannot do: the work of the mind?" [52] A most just and wittily phrased observation. But "sensi-bility," Blackmur's own favorite word, should be sub-stituted for "style" perhaps. For the style is only the

data of the sensibility. Blackmur, for all his greater
sophistication of manner, may be no more consequential
a "thinker" than his fleshier fellow romantic, D. H.
Lawrence. But Blackmur's later criticism succeeds, like
the best of Lawrence's, perhaps because it too is the expression of a sensibility so individual, so alive and instinctive, so perfectly unfettered by "mere head" and rational formulae, and thus so tyrannic and self-sufficient
and free, that the interpretations it delivers have sometimes the surprise and freshness and rightness of virtual
illuminations. One may complain of Blackmur's difficulty
and at times feel imposed upon and even embarrassed by
the style. But there is so much of value even in the later
work—I think, for example, of the essays on *The Idiot*,
on *The Sacred Fount*, on *Madame Bovary*—that perhaps, as Ransom suggests, he may be justly regarded,
nevertheless, as one of the most sensitive and subtle
critics of our time.

chapter 6

Allen Tate: From the Old South to Catholic Orthodoxy

I WANT to characterize Allen Tate, the last and for our purposes most important of the four pilgrims, as the type of the man of letters in the modern world— a designation he seems himself to have sanctioned in the title he gave to a recent collection of his essays. Consider all he has been: Southerner, expatriate (though as a Guggenheim Fellow, the time was right), reactionary, and traditionalist; editor, academician, novelist, biographer, and social commentator; and above all, critic and poet. A few years ago he became also a Roman Catholic. Perhaps T. S. Eliot, who gave to our century the great completing gesture of conversion, is the archetype. But Eliot has more exceptions: his is only a quasi-Catholicism, and though he is a man of letters he has also been content to become something of a business executive, thus accepting one aspect of the split in modern sensibility.

And he has had to acquire his traditions. But Tate was born out of the very ashes of his tradition and in the very place of its conflagration. And he has not only all along kept *in* the modern world, probing it everywhere in the excursions of his dialectic, but has sought engagement with it always in his heroically, sometimes almost tragically conceived capacity as modern man of letters.

Tate has always been less a technical literary critic than an essayist using literature as the frame of reference within which he criticizes the mind and life of his time in the light of his convictions about the proper ends of man. He speaks as a twentieth-century humanist intellectual, isolated and virtually unheard in the barbaric society whose larger deformities it is his concern to examine and minister to. But one can hardly fail to understand his essays also as the battleground of his personal decisions as an individual man and man of letters. He can be seen as the man of letters pursuing through the modern world a typically passionate and difficult pilgrimage in quest of certainty. But his individual direction has been, roughly, to move from the uncertain ideal of the agrarian Old South toward the orthodox actuality of the Church. He made his beginning in the historical idea of a particular "traditional" society because, like the Church to which he finally came, it seemed to provide a myth, a form, a locus of integrity, at least a symbolic footing for the individual mind in a world whose modernity was constituted by intellectual and moral chaos. But this idea, itself the end of an implicit quest, was finally unequal to the forces of the modern chaos. To discover why is also to discover the principle of the necessity of the pilgrimage. Let us begin by understanding the forces as Tate has understood them.

In the preface to *Reason in Madness* Tate addressed himself to "a deep illness of the modern mind." The illness, which has continued to be the object of his critical scrutiny, was what Eliot had called "dissociation of sensibility." It was a condition so pervasive in modern life that the traditional humane ideal of wholeness, whether in man's nature or in society, had become fragmented into chaos, a chaos which could also look like a tyranny. Following Maritain, Basil Willey, and others, Tate has assigned what is at least the typical cause of the illness to Descartes, who, Tate says, isolated "thought" from the rest of man's nature.[1] Tate finds that since Descartes men have chosen more and more to locate their certainties exclusively in "reason" and its practical techniques, called "science." But the positivist-rationalist certainty, which is the characteristically modern one, Tate sees as chimeric and monstrous in that it violates by exclusion those higher potentialities of wholeness that make man's nature human.

Tate's anti-positivism is well known. It is an intellectual aversion he shares with most of his fellow critics and humanists. But he shares it too, as they do, with the poets of the Romantic movement. In an essay on

"Three Types of Poetry" [2] Tate once proposed that after the seventeenth century the pragmatic motive, having separated itself from the rest of man's nature, secured its ascendancy by making its very separateness more and more an accepted principle of thought and action. This meant an inevitable tyranny of means over ends, of fact over knowledge, of intellect over feeling. In revolt against this emergent tyranny of science and rationalism, the Romantics threw away the intellect, handed the feelings to the will, and turned the will, thus driven, irresponsibly loose upon nature. The result was a reactionary condition of mind and art cut loose from the possibility of wholeness and form in the fullest sense.

In a remarkable pair of essays on Dante and Poe—and they should be read together—Tate has demonstrated through contrast the terminal consequences of the Romantic reaction. Dante is the artist of wholeness, and Tate designates his sensibility—in which will, intellect, and feeling function in harmony—as the "symbolic imagination." The symbolic imagination finds in the world of sense and feeling a direction toward a world of idea and spirit, and the symbol it creates is an event of both in simultaneity. Dante's *Divine Comedy* is an action as symbolic discovery: "The symbolic imagination conducts an action through analogy, of the human to the divine, of the natural to the supernatural, of the low to the high, of time to eternity." [3] But if Dante is the poet of this sort of symbolic action, Poe is the poet of

rapt stasis. His is the last condition of the Romantic reaction, in which nature itself, the arena where will is
translated into action and intellect into thought, is finally
abandoned. Poe is the ultimate expression of what Tate
calls the "angelic imagination," which feels itself "quasi-
divine" and "tries to disintegrate or to circumvent the
image in the illusory pursuit of essence." [4] The Me
triumphs over the Not-Me, and the Romantic excess
that D. H. Lawrence called the sin of "*self*-conscious-
ness" issues in an art and philosophy based on a monstrous solipsism. Tate says of *Eureka*, Poe's formulation
of his "metaphysic," that here "every man *is* God: every
man the nonspatial center into which, by a reverse motion of atoms, the universe will contract, as into its annihilation." "Poe as God," Tate writes, "sits silent in
darkness." [5]

Tate would expect us, I think, to understand Poe only
analogically, to translate Poe's yearning for "pure" intellect into the circumstances of our own time as a warning against the direct effects of the sciences on modern
thought and sensibility, and their indirect cultural effect
in, as he describes the theme of his own famous "Ode,"
"the cut-off-ness of the modern 'intellectual man'"
from his modern acquisitive society.[6] But as D. H.
Lawrence demonstrated again and again, and as Tate
also seems to have recognized, what one intends to say
and think is not always the same thing as what one
has "really" thought and said. Tate concludes his essay

on Poe and the "Angelic Imagination" with this warning: "We shall be so exhausted in our liberty that we shall have to take our final rest, not in the cool of the evening, but in the dark, if any one of our modes decides to set up in business for itself." [7] I think it most relevant to understand this warning in the light of its simplest and most obvious relation to Poe as stand-in for the modern man of letters. And that is as a warning to him, as he defends the arts and the whole mind, to resist not only the half-life of an autotelic positivism, but even more its opposite—the solipsistic life-in-death of intellectual inversion.

So we must see the man of letters, then, as flanked dangerously by two opposed chimeras of certainty, two opposed forces of the chaotic modern world that he perceives and must try to survive in. The first of them, positivism, Tate has unmistakably kept clear of. But the second—and, for the man of letters, perhaps inherently the more seductive—has sometimes been harder for him to recognize.

Like the other New Critics, Tate has from the beginning opposed the spirit of romanticism. He has been acutely aware of its dangers to mind as a virtually reflexive gesture of reaction, whether against the traditional past or the positivist present. In an early essay on "Confusion and Poetry" Tate astutely observed that the contention between the "Romantic" critics (he named Van Wyck Brooks, Mencken, Mumford, Spingarn, and the "very young" followers of guerilla William Carlos Williams) and the New Humanists was not a real contention between tradition and contemporaneity or between morality and reality, but rather between rival romanticisms. The two groups, he wrote, were fundamentally the same in that they had both given "allegiance to a single order of values by making a religion of literature;" and he found the only real opposition in a few "skeptical" and "searching" critics like John Crowe Ransom.[8] At the time Tate was also a skeptical and searching critic in much the same sense, by conviction and temperament certainly, as well as by his official loyalties to the Agrarians, *The Fugitive*, and his former mentor, Mr. Ransom. And so he has been since, as his titles tell us: *Reactionary Essays*, *Reason in Madness*, and, if we understand the allusion to Poe, *The Forlorn Demon*.

But the "reaction" has been fierce, and the "reason" darkly interested. An English critic has observed, I think with unfair cleverness, that Tate "wrote poems about not being scientific in a way which reminds one of Wordsworth writing poems about writing poetry."[9] Alfred Kazin wrote more truly in *On Native Grounds* that "what one saw in his work was a rage, so profound and superior a hatred of science and positivism, not to say democracy, that it was almost too deep for words."[10] "Furious" and "rage" were words that once came naturally too to R. P. Blackmur in reviewing a volume of

Tate's poetry.[11] But also "order," which the poems were a way of imposing upon the "chaos" of the reality the poet perceived. One of the major ordering forms envisioned by Tate, in both his poetry and his criticism, has been the idea of the traditional society as tragically because imperfectly realized by the Old South.

The idea of the traditional society was the motif of the fierce reaction and the critical reason both; and to keep intact the metaphor this chapter has been building on, it represented imaginatively the ideal end of the man of letters' pilgrimage through the modern world. To Tate a "traditional society" has meant one whose economy functioned to support a coherent and perpetuable moral code.[12] He envisioned it as a feudal or semi-feudal society rooted in the soil of a particular place and corrected by a universal community of values of which it is a local expression. The idea of the "classical-Christian world," Tate has written, was "based upon the regional consciousness, which held that honor, truth, imagination, human dignity, and limited acquisitiveness, could alone justify a social order however rich and efficient. . . ." [13] The agrarian Old South was only a partial realization of this ideal, and its defects—its failures of religion and art particularly, and the cataclysm of the War—gave it a special piquancy as a symbol: "The South," Tate observed in an essay on "The Profession of Letters in the South," "has had reverses that permit her people to imagine what they might have been. (And only thus can people discover what they *are*.)" [14]

In the same essay, first published in 1935, Tate as a Southerner and man of letters examined the Old South's failure to achieve a high literary culture. The essay's suggestion of what might have been almost becomes a plea to recreate and maintain in the present an actual regional identity in Southern writing, even in publishing. Similarly, in the essay on "Religion and the Old South," originally published in 1930 in *I'll Take My Stand*, Tate's analysis of the Old South's religious failure adumbrated both a social ideal and a personal imperative. His thesis was that the South had lacked a contributing feudal religion to complement its agrarian-feudal social structure. The tone of its religion was "protestant," with which Tate associated the supposed abstractionist-materialist character of the Northern mind. The Southern mind, deprived of an appropriate religion, was condemned to a growth weaker and more fragmentary than the Southern society as a "traditional" or "whole" society promised to evolve. As a consequence, the South expressed itself only through politics—which was "abstractionist" in the Northern fashion. Tate asked himself at the end of the essay how the Southerner could get hold of his tradition now. His answer was, "By violence." It had to be "by violence" because beneath the historical tradition there had been no real and surviving religion for him to fall back on. And "violence" meant, ironically, the abstractionism of an essentially political faith—a faith in reaction, in a return to the feudal-agrarian form of society symbolized by the Old South. "The Southerner is faced with a paradox," Tate wrote in conclusion: "He must use an instrument, which is political, and so unrealistic and pretentious that he cannot believe in it, to re-establish a private, self-contained, and essentially spiritual life. I say that he must do this; but that remains to be seen." [15]

Alfred Kazin has compared Tate's Old South to the Marxist's Russia of the thirties as "an ideal embodied in a culture, a community to be used as a standard of order and fellowship against the Enemy." [16] But the great difference was that Russia, however much its actuality violated the Marxist's ideal, was alive and available as a symbol, while Tate's South was dead. It is in fact a ghostly South that, especially in Tate's poetry, hovers with restless irony about a present perceived by the poet as wasteland or nightmare. Tate has written of Poe, "If he was a madman he was also a gentleman." [17] It may be. But real madness is a nightmare chaos that no mere imaginatively or aesthetically conceived form can long contain. And certainly the manners and morals of the gentleman, the pattern of the social forms and values that we associate with the idea of "civilization," did not very importantly condition Poe's art. If we may once again find implications in the Poe analogy, perhaps one of

them will be that the deeply felt revulsion against positivist modernity that has come to be known as the "Romantic reaction" was similarly too deep and intense to be
checked and formed by a merely provisional secular
faith in the idea of a traditional society.

In 1945 Tate published "The New Provincialism," an
essay which amounts to a kind of leave-taking of that
secular faith, formulated fifteen years earlier at the end
of the essay on "Religion and the Old South." "The
New Provincialism" was written during the Second
World War, under the shadow of its violence and in the
light of the emerging philosophy of One World. The last
remnants of the old orders were being destroyed (compare Tate's poem "To Our Young Proconsuls of the
Air"), and the One World destined to arise was universal
in space but temporally provincial in its total severance
from the past. Tate marked the First World War as
bringing the South back into the modern world. Then
came the "Southern renascence," which, as a "backward
glance," produced "a literature conscious of the past in
the present," a literature informed by the tension between the fact of a chaotic present and the idea of an
ordered traditional past. But now it was as if even that
provisional secular faith could no longer survive. "From
now on," he concluded, "we are committed to seeing
with, not *through* the eye: we, as provincials who do
not live anywhere." [18] Poe as artist had had no status in
his society, no established profession of letters to enable

him to nurture in his art whatever there was in him of the intelligence and civilization of the gentleman. Tate as man of letters had been similarly isolated, and now even the staying symbol of the Old South, itself a kind of talisman against the demon of romanticism, seemed to have been swept way by these newest eruptions of the modern chaos.

A traditionalist without a tradition, an absolutist without absolutes, a religious sensibility without a religion—what could such a man be but a version of romantic? Tate's romanticism has been commented upon in recent years by several writers. Vivienne Koch, for example, has found the original classicism of his poetry giving way more and more to a romantic quality that reaches its climax in "Seasons of the Soul." [19] Another writer has seen in his more recent criticism an "almost Emersonian mysticism," and still another heard in Tate's interpretation of Longinus "the language of the metaphysical idealist, especially Hegel and Croce." [20] A surprising language to find there, since Tate had once spoken with some contempt of the high-sounding "slogans" of art that the New Humanists and "romantic" critics had lifted from Croce and the nineteenth-century Germans, among others. This was in "Confusion and Poetry," [21] where, it will be remembered, Tate had disapproved the same critics for making, in the way of romantics, a religion of literature.

Tate has continually declared his mistrust of quasi-religions of art, especially that of Matthew Arnold, whom he apparently regards as their official sponsor for our century.[22] Yet these declarations have had the interesting quality of perhaps partly conscious and vividly relevant *self*-criticism. For Tate himself can be understood as a maker of art into religion. Alfred Kazin has accused him of turning literature into a series of "isolated ecstasies," in order to save it from science: "Only the poem remained, and its incommunicable significance; and before it the critic worshipped as at a mystic shrine, since it was all human knowledge and all spiritual insight." [23] Professor Francis Roellinger showed some years ago that Arnold's theory of poetry, which Tate had so vigorously attacked in his essay on "Literature as Knowledge" for giving poetry's case away to the sciences, was in the last analysis "not very much different from Mr. Tate's." [24] And Monroe Spears, former editor of *Sewanee Review* and an admirer of Tate, has found that the knowledge supposedly constituted by poetry looked strangely like "the contemplation or vision or revelation of absolute truth sought usually in philosophy and religion." Tate, he says, seemed at times to be "making art a substitute for religion," which results not in a doctrine of art for art's sake, but of "life for art's sake." [25]

The characterization is right and useful. But I should prefer it "art for life's sake" to enforce the Arnoldian likeness that, for all his denials, has been implicit in Tate's view of poetry. The difference from Arnold is one first of tone: where Arnold is respectable, journalistic, and traditionally humane, Tate is tragic, cryptic, mystic; and second of verbal technicalities: where Arnold distinguishes "idea" from mere fact, Tate distinguished "knowledge." And both alike attribute to poetry the higher thing distinguished. In a very early essay called "Poetry and the Absolute" (1927), Tate declared his allegiance to Aristotelian metaphysics and poetics and his opposition to "Romantic German aesthetics through Hegel," which dissolved the concrete experience of poetry into the absolute Absolute. Tate's proposition was that poetry had nothing to do with the absolute-as-substance of metaphysics, but was instead "absolute experience"—meaning, I take it, experience "in itself," unique, unreferential, instransitive.[26] This sounds something like the view of Ransom, who has, of course, nurtured on "Romantic German aesthetics through Hegel." Though Tate attempted to banish the mists of German aesthetics by invoking the weighty name of Aristotle, what threatened to loom up in their place, in spite of the philosophical jargon, was the spectral exoticism of Wilde and Pater. Tate has never reprinted this essay. But it is a useful specimen of the beginnings of Tate's actual romanticism of thought, and helps to explain why in the end, beyond the deep and unforgettable individuality of his rage, his work would finally exhibit a romantic enthusiasm like Coleridge's supported by a romantic moralism like Arnold's.

At many points in his essays one could almost imagine that Tate had consciously set out to complete the work that the romanticisms of Arnold and Coleridge left unfinished. Arnold's attempted exaltation of poetry as increasingly the "consolation and stay" of "the spirit of our race," Tate perfects by returning to poetry the rights to "knowledge" that Arnold was supposed to have signed away to the sciences in such essays as the one on "Literature and Science." And when in "The Man of Letters in the Modern World," Tate asks of "the letter of the poem, the letter of the politician's speech, the letter of the law," "Is there in this language genuine knowledge of our human community—or the lack of it —that we have not had before?"[27] he does for the imagination what Coleridge, its most famous philosophic partisan, was ultimately unable to do. He performs an act of recognition of the imagination as the unifying power not only of artistic creation, but also of man's total life as a spiritual and social being.

Tate has glorified in similar fashion the activity of the critic. Criticism, he has written, expressing through metaphors of mystic intensity an Arnoldian emphasis on the importance of the critical faculty, occupies a "middle position between imagination and philosophy," which makes it "perpetually impossible. Like a man literary criticism is nothing in itself; criticism, like man, embraces pure experience or exalts pure rationality at the price of abdication from its dual nature." [28] Or, to put it another way—and I assume the obviousness of the image Tate has here provided of the man of letters' difficult sojourn between two chimeras of modernist certainty—at the price of the freedom, as well as of the sanity, which is implicit in the idea of an uncommitted and skeptical intelligence.

Since it is as critic, as a voice of "reason" amid the modern madness, or a voice whose reason is as a madness to its surroundings, that the artist becomes the man of letters, I think Tate's conception of criticism and the critic is of special importance in this interpretation of him as an unmistakable if reluctant romantic. Tate has pictured the ideal criticism in a chaotic time as the expression of a "whole" and traditionally formed mind intellectually detached from the present. And I suppose for him its exemplar, besides the "skeptical and searching" Mr. Ransom of Tate's relative youth, would be T. S. Eliot. Such a criticism does the work neither of "reason" nor of feeling and intution, but of "intelligence," which involves both. At its best, he had told us in his note on "The Critic's Business," it is no more nor less than "the ordering of original insights and . . . passing them on, through provisional frames of reference, to other persons secondhand." [29] It should be noted that this detached critical intelligence holds off explicitly from all limiting critical dogmas and methodologies, and implicitly too from the larger dogmas, social and spiritual, that would seek to compel literature into becoming an instrument of something else. This recalls Arnold's continual emphasis on the necessary "disinterestedness" of criticism. But from literature considered as an art the critical intelligence must move into the broader human issues; for literary standards, Tate has observed, "in order to be effectively literary, must be more than literary." [30] And this should recall not only T. S. Eliot, but also Arnold again, who believed that criticism dealt with the best that has been thought and known in the world, and that literature is a "criticism of life," which is much more than a matter of the aesthetics of literature.

I am suggesting that the critical "intelligence" hypostatized by Tate, with the breadth of work that he assigns it, requires and desires, as the romantic mind does, both freedom and certainty. The word "intelligence" presumes to justify the man of letters' keeping free of commitment to any of the formulas of the modern world, whose fragmentation and dehumanization, measured against his vision of the coherent and traditional society, reveal no enabling pattern for full human realization. But it presumes also to reassure by suggesting a sufficient wholeness and certainty of mind—what in much lesser contexts might be called "good sense"—to save him from capsizing in a gust of reaction.

But in spite of the reasonable-sounding rhetoric, the actual position of Tate's man of letters looks untenably paradoxical. Let me quote something strikingly relevant to the point at issue that Tate wrote nearly a generation ago in the essay on "Confusion and Poetry." He had then discovered the New Humanists caught in a telling intellectual dilemma: they desired authority at the same time they desired "freedom from the traditional sources of moral judgment, as these come down to us in living institutions like the church." Their solution, he wrote, was to make "a vague mixture of Classical and Christian authors" into their missing traditional or institutional authority.[31] A solution, is it not, like Tate's own humane critical "intelligence," like Arnold's quest for the best that has been thought and known, and eventually even like Wordsworth's and Coleridge's intuition, which by-passes the discursive books to go straight to infants, peasants, and mountains, Truth's natural vessels? His solution is a romantic solution, and the end it looks toward is the angelized intellect of Poe, where without either nature or light "thought" is its own object, its own substance, its own structure. Some words of Tate's own, abducted into my special context here, supply exactly the suggestive application I wish to make about Tate's position as the man of letters who does not live intellectually anywhere in the modern world. Here are the disturbing last sentences of "Our Cousin, Mr. Poe":

Mr. Poe tells us in one of his simpler poems that from boy-hood he had "a demon in my view." Nobody then—my great-grandfather, my mother, three generations—believed him. It is time we did. I confess that his voice is so near that I recoil a little, lest he, Montressor, lead me into the cellar, address me as Fortunato, and wall me up alive. I should join his melancholy troupe of the undead, whose voices are surely as low and harsh as the grating teeth of storks. He is so close to me that I am sometimes tempted to enter the mists of pre-American genealogy to find out whether he may not actually be my cousin.[32]

Let us come back into the element of our discourse and direct the force of these metaphors upon the man of letters as a free-floating humanistic intelligence scru-tinizing, in the capacity of critic, the discontinuous, de-humanized modern world. What is this intelligence that he would exercise? And how would we know it from a possibly Satanic intelligence? And when it acted criti-cally, would we not be implicitly committed in advance to accepting whatever "insights" came from it labeled as products of a free, unmethodological and undogmatized mind? What *is* an "insight"? How is it different from a logical conclusion or an empirical observation? And how could we tell it from a whim, an error, a lie?

These are rhetorical questions. But they represent, I think, very real problems, unless we are going to take Tate's critical discourse as merely a lifework of idle rhetoric. The man of letters makes assertions about im-

portant matters—about literature, yes, but also about
values generally, about life, about "reality." He engages
with philosophical questions by his own choice, and if
we take any stock in the answers he gives, "provisional"
or not, we must care how well they meet the tests of
experience, of logic, or even of received dogmas. To
care may be our only protection, for all we know,
against a philosophic madness, or a Poeish descent into
the romantic maelstrom, or a hopeless entombment by
Montressor as critic.

It seems, actually, that Tate has become his own Montressor, that in the end he has lain down almost willingly
where he never wanted to—in darkness, with his cousin
Mr. Poe. But there is another act in this drama of the
mind of the man of letters in the modern world. Capitu-
lation to the intellectual anarchy of romanticism would
indeed mean, by the man of letters' own standards, a
kind of tragedy of the mind—or, at the very least, a
death. But Tate became a convert, a few years ago, to
Christianity; and I think we may understand that conversion as a kind of resurrection. There were intimations
as early as 1930 of what the end would be, when Tate
chided the New Humanists in these words: "It is suicidal
to keep the cake of religion and eat it too; . . . you
cannot have religion without *a* religion." [33] And in the
same place Tate quoted, with a little disapproval of the
lack of disinterestedness, the interest in action, a suggestive rhetorical question from Yvor Winters: "Mr. Eliot

has turned Anglo-Catholic; Mr. Tate contents himself
with stating his thesis. . . . One is, however, naturally
moved to wonder, of Mr. Eliot *how* he did it, of Mr.
Tate what he is going to do next." [34] The answer was
finally exhibited when Tate's pilgrimage ended on the
high hard ground of Roman Catholic orthodoxy.

Tate has many times proclaimed the need for absolutes,
knowing at the same time that he himself hadn't any. [35]
And as he seems to have felt the warning in the nightmare sensibility of Poe, he also observed in some of those
around him the various ravages of the formless power of
romanticism—in Ford Madox Ford, for example, and
most tragically in Hart Crane. [36] And there had been Ca-
tholicism in Tate's family—two generations before him
on his mother's side. [37] So the Church was a part of his
ghostly tradition that had survived live and actual into
the present. But he was slow in coming to it. "I am not a
Catholic," he said in 1950, the same year he assented, in
a statement for the *Partisan Review* symposium on religion and the intellectuals, to a tentative Christian belief,
but only through the first sentence of the Athanasian
Creed. [38] So far as it is marked in the essays, the conversion seems to have come about 1951, the year in
which Tate published the pair of essays on Dante and
Poe and the symbolic and angelic imaginations. By 1953
he was urging, quite frankly as a Catholic, that Catholic
literature be truly literary and not merely pious or
doctrinal. [39] In the latter year he was welcomed home by

a writer in *Catholic World* as, along with Mauriac, Eliot, and Graham Greene, a "paradoxical pilgrim," one of the modern Hamlets who had come back to orthodoxy.[40]

The preoccupations of the Agrarian with the Old South as a kind of icon of a reactionary political faith have almost entirely faded from Tate's more recent essays. They will probably remain in his work as a poet, though, where the Old South has all along been serving its best purposes purely as the created and suggestive symbol that it is. And Tate has been publishing in recent years parts of a poem that reflects his new circumstances as a Catholic convert. It is written in the meters of Dante's *Divine Comedy*, and promises to be like that poem in spirit, a work of intense vision and reflection. It is also Tate's first really long poem, which seems to bear out the principle, expressed in his criticism, that only a man with a myth can write one.

In the criticism there is still the mystic fervor, but it is now, presumably, regulated by the structures of the Church and sanctioned by the histories of its saints, and need no longer justify itself with the old humanistic slogans of certainty or the ejaculatory jargon of the romantic intuitionist. And the reactionary rage that has given us some of the most memorable literary essays of our times is still fiercely operative. But now it has a more definite work to do, something in the nature almost of holy war. It is the Christian work of our time, he told a gathering of Catholic intellectuals in Italy in

1955, not simply to fight Russia and Communism, but to fight "the belief in the omnipotence of reason in the political order," and the "omnicompetent state" wherever and in whatever form it may arise.[41]

I think one must take the view that where Tate has finally arrived on his pilgrimage has not been precisely a destination in the sense of an ending. Instead of putting down burdens he has taken up new ones. For, as in the case of Eliot, the place where he has chosen to lay his final allegiance has itself become the origin of a new creative progress. Soon, probably, they will be speaking of the work of the fifties as the beginning of his third period.

PART III

The New Criticism's Mystique of Poetry

> *There is a strong taint of original genius about many critics. . . .*
>
> **R. P. BLACKMUR**

chapter 7

Poetry as Knowledge

ALLEN TATE's conversion, a few years ago, to orthodox Christianity, juxtaposed with his colorful and instinctive romanticism of mind and sensibility, assumes the role, for the modern romantic, of a kind of technical or symbolic salvation from Matthew Arnold. For Arnold had seen the romantic future of poetry and its critics coming, and if you were a commited traditionalist and anti-romantic you had to scorn and fear that vision and the pseudo-religious devotions it implied. Of course one does not convert for literary reasons—that is, to control or thwart one's tendency to turn into a romantic. But one does convert out of felt metaphysical need and a sense of guilt, though sooner or later these may get translated into the intellectual terms of theology and its dependent ethical and political systems. The felt metaphysical need has been strong in the New Criticism, and has tended to express itself largely in the language of attitudes and concepts that the term "romantic" names pretty accurately. Yet the accompanying conscious anti-romantic strain in the New Criticism, with its intellectual allegiance to orthodoxy and the related concept of a traditional and hierarchial society cannot be ignored. With Tate's example shaping our view, this orthodoxy looks like a way of dealing with the "guilt" of romanticism; a way of controlling the romanticism perhaps, but also a way of expiating it: a penance intellectually grasped and willingly undertaken for sins of instinctive sensibility. It appears to me, however, that the orthodoxy, or orthodoxism, of most of the major New Critics has remained only a technical orthodoxy—an escape clause—as far as literary criticism and theory are concerned. The flight from Arnold has ended, ironically, not in the Church's but in Coleridge's bosom, redolent with the auras of laudanum and German Idealism. For the important intellectual sources of the New Criticism have been, for the most part, romantic in nature, as has been its chief intellectual fruit—the doctrine of Poetry as Knowledge.

There is an impressive irony, as Murray Krieger has observed, in the fact of Coleridge's importance to a critical movement that has some of its strongest roots in the anti-romanticism of a T. E. Hulme.[1] Yet even Hulme was subject to some of the Coleridgean attractions, just as most modern critics and theorists have been. The

Biographia Literaria, in the words of Stanley Hyman, "is almost the bible of modern criticism." [2] Perhaps there have been exceptions (I think of F. R. Leavis' feeling that the currency of the metaphysically woolly Coleridge "as an academic classic is something of a scandal"),[3] but both the critics and their commentators have confirmed Hyman's view by recognizing Coleridge as the older authority to whom most of them are most indebted. Professor R. S. Crane, reasonably, it seems to me, considers Eliot, Brooks, Ransom, and Tate to be "Coleridgean" in important ways right along with I. A. Richards.[4] And though he is not given to citing Coleridge, Blackmur's theory and practice as well as his early appreciative essay on the criticism of Herbert Read, an enthusiastic Coleridgean, suggests that he too ought to be added to the list.[5]

This central importance of Coleridge widens, on further examination, into an encompassing importance for the New Criticism of philosophical Idealism generally. Students have found Idealistic influences in the works of Brooks, Tate, Ransom, and Wellek and Warren, as well as in some of the contemporary aestheticians related to the New Criticism, such as Vivas, Mrs. Langer, and Theodore M. Greene.[6] Among New Critics openly avowing Idealistic debts we think first, of course, of I. A. Richards, who in his latest collection of essays seems to make Plato—ostensibly for his "method"—almost as important a personal authority as Coleridge has been.

Ransom's debt specifically to modern Idealism is weighty: he admits to having learned from the "Neo-Hegelians," and traces Richards' "conversion" to them; [7] he recalls his own "literary speculations" outgrowing Aristotle ("by that time I had at least read Kant and Croce"), [8] and affectionately refers to Kant as "my own mentor"; [9] and he seems virtually to equate the word "philosophy" with the philosophy of the romantic movement when, in the essay on "The Concrete Universal," he declares Wordsworth, Coleridge, Keats, Shelley, and Byron a "first-rate sequence of poets" thanks to their having had poetry conceived philosophically. [10]

Blackmur, who, in spite of what appear to be frequent philosophical borrowings, rarely cites non-literary sources, has made admiring reference to intuitionist-expressionist Croce, [11] with whom Ransom says "the modern criticism came in," [12] and appears to owe in addition a general debt of theory at least to Bergson, Santayana, and Whitehead. [13] Eliseo Vivas records, finally, in the preface to *The Moral Life and the Ethical Life*, that at the time of his revulsion against positivistic Naturalism he "swallowed fast and greedily" a new philosophical diet, including Kant and Bergson, as well as Kierkegaard, Cassirer, and some saints and novelists. [14] He urges elsewhere against the Chicago Aristotelians that the imitation theory of art has been insufficient ever since Schelling, the Schlegels, and "idealistic philosophy" generally. [15] And he admits that his own doctrine of art as "creation and discovery" is a version of "the purely speculative Kantian hypothesis that the mind is . . . constitutive of our ambient world." [16]

This small sampling of opinions and avowals has been offered only to suggest introductorily why it is that the philosophy of poetry about to be examined, the New Critic's doctrine that Poetry is Knowledge, is romantic in substance and mood. While philosophical Idealism has perhaps contributed most to the development of the doctrine, I do not mean to suggest that its origins lie exclusively with Coleridge and the Germans. The New Critics have never been philosophically systematic, and they have often interested themselves also in contemporary romantic-like philosophies, primitivist, mystical, religiose—most of them perhaps Idealist-related or Idealist-derived. But the point of the discussion to follow will not be to trace origins or to anatomize their ends, but rather to exhibit the Poetry-as-Knowledge doctrine as an *un*orthodox, perhaps *anti*-orthodox, romantic dogma implicitly in support of a quasi-religion of poetry.

The work of John Crowe Ransom, philosopher general to the New Criticism now for many years, has been consistent in its devoutly "speculative" inquiry into the nature of poetry. For practically the whole of Ransom's critical career has been devoted to elucidating and refining that doctrine through his structure-texture trope and its eventual restatement in the idea of the Concrete

Universal. But Ransom has not stood still. He has himself taken, in fact, a small pilgrimage toward Truth along with some of his fellow critics. For I think that "texture" and particulars tended to have the main emphasis in his earlier essays, with "structure" and universals, as the necessary complementary values, carrying relatively more weight in the essays after the thirties. "Plato, Aristotle, the Hegelians, and many others related and unrelated," Ransom complained in *The World's Body*, "are quite alike in being unable to attach their interest to mere particulars, and disposed always to use them as the beginnings of a process destined to go 'higher,' 'behind,' or 'further.' . . ." [17] This is an early statement of Ransom's general reaction against the abstraction of "uses," whether philosophical or pragmatic, from nature. And it would have specific application in criticism, obviously, to habitual critical and pedagogical quests for the moral and the meaning of the poem as sufficient ends.

It was against abstractionism in this sense that Ransom initiated his campaign in behalf of particulars, of nature as object to be beloved for itself, of poetry or art as the flesh of experience filling out to completion the otherwise merely skeletal knowledges of science and conceptualization. Thus the notion that poetry discovers and provides "the world's body." This is a metaphor based on the stock romantic polarity of science and poetry—*the* metaphor, in fact, that had come so naturally to

Wordsworth as he composed his prefatory remarks to *Lyrical Ballads:* "If the time should ever come," he wrote, "when what is now called science . . . shall be ready to put on, as it were, a form of flesh and blood, the Poet will lend his divine spirit to aid the transfiguration. . . ." The body supplied by poetry Ransom came to call "texture," and the conceptual skeleton which it clothed and animated he called "structure." By the structure of a poem Ransom meant its meaning—its plot, its theme, its "paraphrasable content"—along with its machineries of continuity and organization. By texture he meant all the engaging inclusions of the poem's art—its sound, its rhythm, its images—that interest us aesthetically after they have made whatever structural contribution they are capable of.[18]

Intellect very naturally got associated with structure, and feeling, as might be expected therefore, with texture. Ransom seemed to be trying to straddle this archetypal romantic split between feeling and intellect when he claimed, in *The New Criticism*, that for Coleridge images and feelings "are synonymous . . . in so far as they are one-to-one correspondents, one representing the cognitive side and the other the affective side of the same experience."[19] This means that though an image may be said to be a cognition in that it "corresponds" to something in the real world and is in that sense "true," as Ransom put it elsewhere,[20] it also engages our affections for itself on its own terms as a valuable object of sense experience over and above its service as a cognition.

Most simply, then, an image or a poem may be both an object *understood* and an object *loved*. But since prose or scientific utterance—all discourse other than poetic—is by definition intended and taken as cognitive utterance, and since its importance depends so exclusively upon what Ransom calls "structure" as ideally to exclude any intrusion of texture, texture becomes by logical default the defining characteristic of poetry.[21] It is likewise this "great residue of content which escapes the net of organic analysis," as Ransom once put it, that differentiates the poem from its meaning as "mere paraphrase." [22] If texture makes the substantive difference, obviously feeling is going to make the psychological difference. Feeling—the psychological correspondent of texture—is going to be the distinctive poetic faculty to the relative exclusion of intellect as the prose faculty. Poetry, Ransom wrote in 1947, is "discourse in the 'pathetic mode' if we emphasize the feelings which attend it, but let us say loosely that it is in the 'substantival mode' if we emphasize the character of the referents." [23] This seems to me very close to an open admission, softened by the nervous second clause, that Ransom's texture-structure theory inevitably implies the stock romantic split between poetry-and-feeling on the one hand and prose-and-intellect on the other.

But frankness alone is not enough to take care of two troublesome problems that necessarily arise from the texture-structure account of poetry's nature. The New Critics, and Ransom is no exception, have all along opposed themselves, with an almost moral fervor, to enforced sensibility-splitting of any sort. Nor have they been willing to accept poetic theories that handed knowledge to the sciences—as Tate once claimed the theories of Richards and Charles Morris did in our century, along with Arnold's and Coleridge's in the last—leaving poetry with rights and duties pertaining only to stirring and satisfying the emotions. Ransom has shared with his fellow critics the desire to defend poetry's right to call itself "knowledge," and in his later criticism he implements that desire by merging his texture-structure metaphor with the idea of the "Concrete Universal." This is a rhetorical maneuver that seems to resolve dangerous dichotomies into unity and to restore to poetry an important share in the structure-knowledge-intellect cluster of values. Yet the poetry-as-knowledge doctrine has to be founded on a principle of uniqueness or else, as Francis Roellinger pointed out about Ransom's poetics as of 1941, poetry as knowledge-through-particularity simply "becomes philosophy or science in concrete form" and "the attempt to assign an independent knowledge function to poetry breaks down." [24]

Ransom's earlier defense of poetry as knowledge, with texture as poetry's differentia, had begun with the proposition that scientific discourse gives us "reduced, emasculated, and docile versions" of the world. Poetry, on the other hand, "intends to recover the denser and more refractory original world which we know loosely through our perceptions and memories. By this supposition it is a kind of knowledge which is radically or ontologically distinct." [25] The strong objection to this was, to cite Roellinger again, that "surely poetry must be a poor substitute for what our senses tell us much more immediately." [26] The notion of the Concrete Universal is exactly the sort of refinement—whether or not it succeeds is another question—that attempts not only to claim a knowledge function for poetry, but to avoid objections to that claim by urging the *uniqueness* of poetry and the consequent independence of its knowledge function from philosophy, science, and common sense.

Ransom had the beginnings of his later theory even in the days when he was more willing to simplify his poetics into an attitude of sentimental regard for prosodic effects and postveridical particulars of verbal reference. We find him saying in one of the earlier essays, for example, that the "pure and perfectly contingent details" gratuitously present in most poems—apart from whatever truth to nature the images among them may have—"*stand for* an inexhaustible particularity" (my italics).[27] In his 1940 comment on the language theories of Charles Morris, Ransom translated the implications of the "stand for" into more technical language when he wrote that the "aesthetic icon denotes a body whose structure is intended to denote the structure of the whole world of 'possible' or 'existential' objects." [28] In "Criticism as Pure Speculation" (1941) Random moved still closer to proclaiming the Concrete Universal, for the "speculation" his title referred to concerned the *relation* in poetry between texture and structure as parts of a whole rather than as discrete and logically separable applications of language generally.[29] And in the amalgam of the Kantian Concrete Universal, which is the principle that informs Ransom's more recent work,[30] it is the *relation* of particular to universal that constitutes the knowledge uniquely supplied by poetry.

As the final form of Ransom's theory goes, to state it briefly, the affectively interesting particulars of a poem have the same relation of residual logical irrelevance to its structure ("meaning," plot, meter, and the mechanics of their organization) as nature's particulars (the infinite variations of form, color, species) have to *its* structure (the machinery of energy and "matter," or perhaps the metaphysical finalities). The poem is itself a world "in little." And whether its subject be toads or angels, it *presents*, in the actualized relation between idea and detail, *ontological* knowledge of the world at large— knowledge in the sense that a presumably true abstraction about the nature of reality could be based upon it.

Every true poem, as itself a world in little, is thus an instance of universal ontology presented and exemplified in a local concretion.[31]

If this account of Ransom's later poetics is accurate, then Winters' old charge of "hedonism," [32] and Herbert Muller's that Ransom talks like an "aesthete of the 'nineties," [33] whatever their truth once, would seem now not to have very much point. Of course the hardened philosophical skeptic might still feel that Ransom's final version of the poetry-as-knowledge doctrine, like so much metaphysical discussion, solves an imaginary problem by a shift of grammar—the conversion of the texture-structure noun-noun duality into the Concrete Universal's adjective-noun unity. But my interest here is not in the "truth" of Ransom's speculations, but in their illustration of where the search for a suitable theory of poetry as knowledge is likely to lead when the knowledge is not to be prose knowledge—either scientific or, in the words of a critic of the New Critics, "common knowledge, of things that everyone incipiently knows, or has overlooked, or forgotten." [34] Even if you begin as Ransom did with a respect and a love for particulars, you seem to get drawn in the footsteps of Aristotle, Plato, the Hegelians—and of course the great Romantic poets and theorists of the last century—where in the beginning you may have especially wanted *not* to go: "higher," or "further," or "behind"—or even, like Blackmur, "below."

Most of the New Critics, when bent upon theorizing about the cognitive nature of poetry, have taken, like Ransom, extra-particular journeys toward their ends, though they have employed different verbal vehicles in doing so. Several share with Ransom the general conviction that poetry provides ontological knowledge. Wellek and Warren in *Theory of Literature*, for example, and Cleanth Brooks, after them, accept the Kantian notion that there is a "structure of norms within reality," and that the poem makes it known by organic concretion in an actual experience.[35] Blackmur, too, seems to hold the ontological view. But perhaps because he has gone searching below rather than above, reality for him has more to do with turbulent and clashing forces than with neatly structured norms. According to Blackmur, "executive form," which is art, and I summarize from the essay on "The Loose and Baggy Monsters of Henry James," has the business of providing "an instance of the feeling of what life is about," of making felt the underlying "deep" form of life, which is the force of the waywardness and turbulence of reality pushing against the ordering efforts of mind and conscience.[36] Leslie Fiedler has provided a slightly more decorous version of the same faith by asserting that the function of "mythos" (poetry) as "an immediate intuition of being" is to mediate "between the community and the individual, the person and his fate, the given and the achieved." [37]

Poetry as ontological knowledge seems to shade off,

for Blackmur and Fiedler, toward a second epistemological category—axiological knowledge, knowledge of the
sort talked "about" in the prose of religious, moral, and
aesthetic precept, but presented in poetry as actual experience. "Poetry . . . is knowledge," writes Robert
Penn Warren; not "by report," nor "as symptom" of an
age, but "knowledge by form. No, knowledge *of*
form." [38] And for Allen Tate "works of literature . . .
are the recurrent discovery of the human communion
as experience, in a definite place and at a definite time." [39]
The disvalues in the contexts of both of these quotations
add up to materialism and secularized democracy. Perhaps we have the frankest and simplest statement of what
this category may amount to when Richards, in one of
his more recent essays, seems to echo Eliot by making
the old-fashioned sounding declaration that the humanities in general exist to cultivate "wisdom." [40]

The third type of poetry-as-knowledge theory is
harder to name. It is essentially a theory of poetry as
psychological knowledge. And though "psychological"
is now too drearily clinical a word to convey the mood
of esoteric excitement in which its proponents speak, the
theory is actually of a somewhat humbler order than
the ontological and axiological ones so far described. I
think Suzanne Langer's theory of poetry (or art) as
psychological knowledge is at once the most imaginative
and the simplest of the three theories to be mentioned
here. An art work, Mrs. Langer tells us in *Feeling and*

Form, reveals some "nameless felt passage of 'felt life,' knowable through its incarnation in the art symbol even if the beholder has never felt it in his own flesh." [41] The principle stated in this quotation undergoes, in *Feeling and Form*, innumerable translations, clarifications, elaborations, and circular justifications. For the theme from beginning to end of Mrs. Langer's book, a theme presented first in the earlier *Philosophy in a New Key*, is that art presents for conscious perception and examination in objectified forms events of the subjective life—the life of "feeling" undergone but not understood, feeling perhaps wholly subconscious, even incipient, or even only potential. In short, art presents knowledge of the submerged psychological life.

Vivas is less clear and consistent than Mrs. Langer, but at the same time somewhat less ambitious in his claims for art. His assertion that the arts create and discover our values appears only to be a way of saying, if we read him carefully, that they sharpen, awaken, and alert us spiritually. "What literature . . . gives us," Vivas writes in the essay on "Literature as Knowledge," "is a symbolic construct of what life ought to be like in order to answer the demands of aesthetic apprehension of it"; and he is openly opposed to too presumptuous uses of the word "knowledge" in descriptions of the nature and function of literature.[42] Literature's purpose and function is not quite to *give* knowledge, but to *prepare* us for knowledge. His theory seems to be that successful experiencing of art works as aesthetically ordered complexes of details brings us to a psychological vantage point where "beyond them we perceive an authentic vision of the structure of reality." [43] If we take the "beyond" seriously, and I think in fairness to his intentions we must, Vivas' conception of poetry as knowledge adds up to a kind of contextual pragmatism. Poetry is not quite, in his theory, an analogue of reality; but the intrinsic ordered functioning of its parts has the effect, as the early Richards might have put it, of "ordering" our minds in preparation for something else—an access, perhaps, of some sort or other of *real* knowledge. But for Vivas a poem's "truth"—its "meaning"—seems to be no more than a synonym for the organic coherence of its language: "Poetic language does not merely refer to something through it, and hence external to it, but in it; and hence in some sense its meaning has its locus in the language itself." [44]

Philip Wheelwright's conception of "poetic truth" is very much the same as Vivas'. But it is even less concerned—concerned almost not at all, in fact—with the realms of being beyond poetry to which poetry is the preparatory psychological porch or gateway. "A poetic utterance," he writes in *The Burning Fountain*, "invites our imaginative assent, which is to say our depth assent, to some degree or other and in some context or other." [45] By "depth assent"—one of his key terms is "depth-interest"—he seems to mean intuitive grasp and acceptance, which is "deeper" and more fundamental than rationally or empirically derived assent to a proposition. But Wheelwright speaks of all this as a matter of subjective experience, and stresses that since these moments of depth-assent relate to specific contexts and occasions they may be assumed to be cognitively unrelated to the real world outside those contexts and occasions. It seems, finally, that in Vivas' theory, and certainly in Wheelwright's, the almost exclusively contextual-physchological stress yields a theory not really of poetry as knowledge at all, but of poetry as the occasion and cause of arational *feelings* of insight and illumination.

I have no doubt that valid enough cases could be made against the way I have categorized these theories of poetry as knowledge, and perhaps even against the expositions I have given of them. But the speculative nature of the critics' subject and the instability of their terms would make some distortion and inconclusiveness inevitable, even if everybody brought the same articles of faith to the discussion. Yvor Winters was once very understandably baffled by the use of "cognition" in Ransom's criticism, for example. When applied to "the rational activities of scientists and philosophers," he observed, it tends to be "a term of disparagement"; but when applied to the arts "its meaning is different and to myself is very obscure." [46] Perhaps there is some reason to believe with Murray Krieger that little is accomplished by "the insistence on calling this product of

poetry by the honorific name of *knowledge*." [47] Richards, with C. K. Odgen, pointed out many years ago in
The Meaning of Meaning that critics will often write
"true" of a work of art "where alternative symbols
would be 'convincing' in some cases, 'sincere' in others,
'beautiful' in others, and so on." [48] Richards also explained psychologically how this substitution of terms
happens to take place:

Any state of mind in which anyone takes a great interest
is very likely to be called "knowledge," because no other
word in psychology has such evocative virtue. If this state
of mind is very unlike those usually so called, the new
"knowledge" will be set in opposition to the old and praised
as of a superior, more real, and more essential nature. [49]

We have seen our traditionalist men of letters defend-
ing the arts, in a time of overwhelming positivism, as
embodying vital knowledge supplementary or complementary or proprietary to the knowledges of reason and
science. The picture is dramatic, and from Richards'
perspective makes very tight psychological sense. But as
Krieger has observed, the term "knowledge," at least in
the present state of theory, is just a name "applied to an
admittedly preconceptual affair simply because the term
is so soothing to the self-confidence of the harassed
humanist." [50] It would seem indeed that psychological
need has bred in our New Critics, as it did in the
Romantics of the last century, both philosophical
enthusiasm and rhetorical adventuring.

chapter 8

Criticism as Poetry

THIS chapter will scrutinize a selection of rhetorical examples typical, and usually in some further way illuminating or interesting, of the romantic nature of the New or New-related modern critic. Here we shall get more into the immediate texture of his experience as an apologist for poetry in a positivistic world. I use the word "texture" intentionally to echo Ransom because, since he uses it in his earlier criticism to signal the defining characteristic of poetry, it prepares for the proposition that when "thought" fails or is found inadequate in an urgent cause, poetry—in the sum of its senses from rhetoric to magic—is very likely to take over the job. I would contend that a large part of what we call New Criticism has been written under the influence of the Muses. For in pursuing their defense of poetry the

New Critics have tended to regard appeals to logic and experience, at least on any sort of rigorously formal basis, as from the start tactically inadvisable, or fruitless, or even perverse. They have generally preferred to use essentially *a*logical means of moving and persuading, means that positivists and semanticists crudely call "appeals to emotion" and that literary people respect as the very fruits of craft. By examining some of the machineries of the critics' rhetoric, the sorts of "appeals to emotion" they make, and the dominant categories of the auxiliary imagery they use in their discourse, we shall be seeing at close range instances of the romantic substance and life of their minds both as individual critics and as spokesmen for a cause larger than themselves. I must confess, of course, that my own selection is itself an imposition of rhetoric upon unsuspecting, if not precisely innocent, material.

I think what is to follow can be usefully taken in terms of this somewhat Ransomian image: as a kind of rhetorical oratorio, unified by a chorus of like sentiment and principle and varied by occasional virtuoso voices lifted in aria, with my own comments as recitative and continuo. Let us begin the performance at the intellectual end of the critics' art, discovering first some of their rhetorical maneuvers in behalf of "thought," and then proceed to its more poetic offices, the inducement of pieties and the creation of exemplary images of the nature of poetry.

THE RHETORIC OF SPECULATION

The rhetorical categories to be mentioned in this first section are fairly familiar features of standard metaphysical discourse. In the manner of the great critics of the past, perhaps especially the Romantics, the New Critics have tended to think of poetry and speculative philosophy as closely related, as approaching the same high-level or ultra-real Reality from opposite directions, meeting finally, perhaps, in religion. It seems only appropriate, therefore, that the critics should sometimes talk in the style of metaphysicians. But they are primarily men of letters, and so in the end their interests are going to be involved less in abstract than in substantive discourse. This rhetoric of speculation, then, should be regarded as a discourse merely supporting or preparatory to the poetry of Poetry to come.

1. *Big Words.* Since it is well known that metaphysical speculation begins and ends with big words—Idea, the Good, Logos, Substance, Being, Soul, Flux, the One—it is probably not necessary to provide very many examples of some of the same and similar words from the writings of the New Critics. There have been a good many in earlier quotations, furthermore, and additional instances will appear in the materials of other sections of this chapter. But it may be fitting to consider what the justification is for labeling these words—particularly the great controlling nouns of metaphysical speculation

—as a rhetorical category. I would observe, first of all, that metaphysics necessarily "begins" with the words: in that the point of the philosopher's whole labor is to define them. And when his definitions conflict with those of some other philosopher, the speculative defining will turn into controversy, with the words themselves, since by their very nature they lack determinate referents, becoming the objects of vigorously combative *rhetorical* interest. So whatever the outcome, the controversy will end as it began, with words rather than "facts"—with a situation of equilibrium or tension created by rhetoric rather than by "logic" or "science," though these may have been contributory.

In our time the type of controversy itself, whether in philosophy or in criticism, has become an object of rhetorical interest, as well as of close logical and empirical scrutiny. In criticism the skeptics, like the early Richards, accuse the believers of "logical animism" [1] and "bongus entities," [2] and the believers, represented by Ransom, say, plead for "a degree of speculative fury" in the literary discussions of such self-limited rationalists as the Chicago Aristotelians.[3] We shall see much speculative fury and the free naming of many entities, bogus or not, in the quotations soon to follow. Some of the entities will be named by the big words of general philosophy (Man, Reality, Being), but more often by the big words of the arts and speculative psychology: the Mind, Knowledge, Imagination, Poetry, sometimes Beauty, and of course the classic jargon of the Faculties—Feeling, Will, and Intellect. But what is most important is that they stand for the largest and most crucial concerns of criticism, that they have a broad and uncertain—perhaps even a sliding—reference, that they indeed often seem to refer to entities artificed by hypostatization, and that their use by critics, while reverent in spirit, is most casual and free in the actual pursuit of argument.

2. *The Rhetoric of Definition.* I speak of the "rhetoric" of definition because the efforts of the critics to define the big words, like those of the metaphysicians, often end not in specifying and clarifying but in incanting and evoking. Such definitions function mainly to create a sense of intuited and perhaps unutterable comprehension which, if rhetorically successful, actually *protects* the big word from reduction or translation or redefinition into the small words of common sense. It might be maintained that they are not definitions at all, at least that they have neither the intention nor the effect of definitions as normally understood.

The definitions to follow are those of big words, or of ordinary words elevated or inflated by the definition into big words. And they are all drawn from the work of R. P. Blackmur, the chief practitioner among New Critics of the rhetoric of definition. Where in the work of a critic like Tate such definitions are rarer and more formal, in Blackmur's, perhaps because he is the most indefatigably "speculative" critic we have, they are prolific in numbers, casual and sudden in occurrence, often gorgeous in the language of their formulation. But though Blackmur is the soloist here, the same kind of song is sung in fainter voices by other New Critics as well.

Here is Blackmur on morals: "Morals is what we think about in our quarrel with behavior. . . ." If we inquire what he means by behavior, we find that "behavior is what upsets morals," [4] and that "behavior is the medium in which our lives take place." [5] A related concept, from another essay, is conscience: "Conscience is the bite of things known together, in remorse and in incentive; conscience is that unification of the sense of things which is moral beauty. . . ." [6] And reason will be re-called from an earlier chapter as "the whole mind, the residual form of all we have been, and the conceiving matrix of all that we may become . . . , a servant, the housekeeper who keeps things going by criticism, by philosophy, by art." [7] Turning to the arts, "Critique is the wiggling extreme articulation of vital elements into an order of vision. . . ." [8] And Blackmur's definition of symbol in "Notes on Four Categories in Criticism," of which I here reproduce only a part, is a veritable hymn recalling to most readers, no doubt, like passages from Coleridge:

Symbol is the most exact possible meaning, almost tauto-logically exact, for what stirred the words to move *and* what the moving words made. Symbol stands for nothing previously known, but for what is "here" made known and what is about to be made known. If symbol stands for anything else than itself continuing, it stands for that within me the reader which enables me to recognize it and to illuminate it with my own experience at the same moment that what it means illuminates further corridors in my sense of myself.[9]

In all these passages it should be noted that the definitions call upon the services of additional big words— "unification of the sense of things," "moral beauty," "mind," "morals" and "behavior" alternating as each other's defining reference, and the resonant relative pronouns of the last passage that seem relative to nothing —words that bring with them additional requirements, perhaps, of definition.

3. *Mixed Terms.* Here we come upon another well-known feature of speculative philosophy and criticism, the mixing of terms—an indulgence sanctioned and encouraged by the type of definition we have just examined. The procedure in simplified form is to take a big word like *reason*, perhaps having already robed it with an enlarging speculative definition, and then apply it surprisingly in contexts where the habits of ordinary discourse would lead the normal reader to expect words of unrelated, perhaps even opposite, common sense meanings. We have already seen how, in the essay called "The Language of Silence," Blackmur does this with *reason*, making it a coordinate or an equivalent of

"feeling" as well as of "meter" and "rhythm." [10] And in the essay proposing "Language as Gesture" [11] both of the key terms are expanded so that we know that the key phrase they appear in does not refer to "sign language," any more than "gesture" alone means muscular movement or "language" alone means words in syntax. "Language" and "gesture" are pushed respectively toward the common senses of the words "intuition" and "expression," two words that seem to refer to the subjective and objective way of looking at the same aspect of psychological experience. The words thus get "mixed" in the same meaning. And the phrase "language as gesture" is translatable finally to mean the sentence, "Language (qualified perhaps by 'some' or 'imaginative') *is* gesture," or "Language *equals* gesture," with the implication ensuing that "gesture" is logically substitutable in the contexts where "language," as qualified, would be the key term. Perhaps the most marked example of the rhetoric of mixed terms in the New Criticism is in the doctrine—advanced most consciously in the work of Tate and Ransom—of poetry as knowledge, with "knowledge" undergoing about the same process of fusion just schematized for "gesture."

Sometimes the sort of terminological mixing we have been discussing is the result of mere carelessness. But most often—as in the work of our critics—it is a conscious rhetorical shift, often having the appearance of "argument," designed to deliver some effect or insight outside the capabilities of normal usage. We can perhaps see a positive sign of the rhetorical nature of these maneuvers in the fact that unequal marriages of terms are often the result. Though "language" remains the stronger term, "gesture" seems to gain influence by association with it. But "knowledge," I am afraid, is required to bring all its value to the marriage with "poetry," without being allowed to retain any of the real rights of meaning upon which its value was originally founded: poetry is said to be "cognitive" without giving cognitions *of* anything. But in any case such maneuvers may indeed create the insight or feeling of insight they are intended to create. Or they may, of course, merely irritate close-reading skeptics like Louis Grudin, who some years ago saw an anarchy in Eliot's critical terms, a "dialectical irresponsibility . . . characteristic . . . of the futility of most current critical writing." [12]

4. *Intellectual Punning and Echo with Variation.* These are two minor refinements on the technique of mixing terms, refinements that are virtually the exclusive property of R. P. Blackmur. These rhetorical maneuvers are exercised mostly incidentally, and with less basic and formal terms, in order to give insight in passing. Both techniques imply the larger category of epigram, a classic insight-giving technique ubiquitously evident in Blackmur's work.

Intellectual punning may take many forms. But here

are four examples that may be different enough to imply distinct "types" of intellectual puns. The straight pun (the force of reality "is what bears us and what we cannot bear") [13] merges with the multiple pun ("gesture is that meaningfulness which is moving, in every sense of that word: what moves the words and what moves us").[14] Then there are combinative puns ("the passion of the [Emma Bovary's] reach becomes the compassion of the symbol") [15] and the related separative pun, illustrated in Tate's derivation of his term "tension," as the synthetic truncation of the terms *extension* and *intension*, and puns that after a moment turn out really to be slant rhymes with implied puns submerged in them (the ideas "in James . . . occupy a precarious but precious place").[16]

Echo with variation, also peculiar to Blackmur's work, has the same ability as intellectual punning to provide, by unexpectedly transmuting the known, a medium for insight and sudden illumination. A technique of irony found in poetry of the metaphysical sort, it is a way of "packing" utterance and of forging coherence of meaning out of disparity and incoherence. One Shakespearean example from Blackmur should suffice as comment upon the others: "Behavior is all, even when false." [17] Here a new epigram is born out of an old—insight bred upon insight.

5. *"Dialectic."* There are two senses of this term. The first sense refers to the form of free intellectual conversa-

tion that clever Socrates imposed upon the innocents that crossed his path. It is a sense now more or less in vogue to designate with approval the unsystematic and indeterminate theoretical explorations of most of the New Critics. And because it has humane connotations, it is itself a useful rhetorical tool—backed by the good name of Plato—with which to justify in the face of scientism and pragmatism the speculative "essay" that considers and perhaps proposes without attempting to prove or enforce.

The second sense, our principal concern here, refers to the dialectic of opposites, a rhetorical action of discourse in which the manipulator is free either to force the merging of black and white into some shade of grey, or else to enable his favorite entirely to subdue or absorb its opposition. The rhetoric of dialectical opposition has not only the virtue of restricting the area of battle, and its participants, to practical limits, but also of excluding beforehand a great many vantage points from which hostile attacks might be launched: actual complexity and multiplicity are reduced to an artificial and more easily manipulatable duality.

Poetry vs. Science, Intellect vs. Feeling (sometimes Emotion), Reason vs. Imagination—these are some of the major strands of dialectical opposition woven in and out of the texture particularly of New Criticism. These and other sets of similar opposites are expressions of the larger dialectical principle underlying the doctrine of

Poetry as Knowledge—the principle, as it is called by Kathleen Nott, of "Two Truths." [18] "The issue is one of fact," Ransom claims in *God Without Thunder*. "Is the actual universe amenable to the laws of science, or is it not? Of course the truth is that it partly is, and partly isn't." [19] The Two Truths—that of science and the intellect, and that of religion and the imagination—follow from Ransom's premise, and embody themselves in two sorts of discourse. According to Ransom it is a matter, roughly, of universals versus particulars, with "generalization" as "the fundamental act of science." [20] Ransom sees the Fall of Adam and Eve as a symbolic "first instance . . . of the conflict between science and religion, as they sought for the favor of the human mind." [21] Leslie Fiedler, apparently following Ransom, has associated "the sense of reverence and astonishment . . . which alone breeds *pietas*" with religious-imaginative truth, while "the scientific knowing is a knowledge without love, a rape of nature." [22]

Already the dialectical struggle can be seen as unequal. Religious-imaginative truth is clearly deeper or higher—sacrosanct; and scientific-intellectual truth is lesser, and therefore when, upstart or dominant, evil. Accusations of villainy proceed from the better side: Eliseo Vivas cries out against "Scientism," by which he means "the unempirical faith that science can give us a complete philosophy for all our human needs"; [23] it is all or nothing, he tells us—either ideal moral norms, or else "the frankly 'might-makes-right' morality of the positivist." [24] Ransom is more suave as he imagines "Science" putting religionists through an inquisition: "Do you propose to have a whole Sabbath day lost to human usefulness? Do you intend to require ceremonial rites that cost human labor and wealth, and consume valuable time?" [25] Restrictions and expulsions follow hard upon the accusations: "There is nothing 'escapist,'" writes Cleanth Brooks, "about a hostility to science which orders science off the premises as a trespasser when science has taken up a position where it has no business to be." [26] And so, with science off the premises, or at the very most in the kitchen, the dialectical exhibition is over and religious-imaginative truth reigns supreme.

There are, of course, various lesser or ancillary dialectical procedures in the corpus of the New Criticism—Ransom's texture-structure opposition, for example, which is a rhetorical mechanism for characterizing or defining poetry—that have little or nothing to do with "propaganda." An interesting minor dialectic, expressive of deep and moving currents in its author's subjective experience, is R. P. Blackmur's real-actual opposition, a dialectic that plays through a great many of his later essays. In the "Notes on Four Categories in Criticism," where alone I count forty occurrences of actual-words and fifteen of real-words, it seems that *actual* means "accident," "event," or "matter-in-flux" (or what might more commonly be called "real"),

while *real* means Real in the Idealist's sense—"ideal,"
or "universal." "The arts exemplify the actual," is
Blackmur's proposition here.[27] From his rather imaginative intuitions about Emma Bovary's inserting her
tongue in the cordial glass and the effect of her action on
Bovary, one gathers Blackmur's point to be that art
makes accidents or particulars into exemplars of universals through symbolization.[28] Thus art makes the actual
"real" in the sense roughly of "ideal."

Elsewhere this explanation of the meaning of the real-
actual dialectic does not work. In the essay on "Four
Quartets" there seem to be two distinct senses of real in
opposition to actual ("Man dwells in the actual, between
the real and the real"), only one of which is clearly
related to the object of what he calls "ideal aspiration." [29]
And in the essay on "The Loose and Baggy Monsters of
Henry James," though at one point "spiritual" and
"sensual" are respectively paired with "ideal" and
"actual," [30] "real" seems finally to mean so much that it
means nothing, when Blackmur writes that Strether's
self-denial in *The Ambassadors* "was a gesture of this
ideal [of 'rightness'], and it could have been otherwise,
could in another soul have been the gesture of assent;
for the beauty and the knowledge were still there, and
the reality, which contains both the ideal and the actual,
and so much more, stands, in its immensity, behind." [31]
The dialectic has been wholly eluded, and the terms have
wholly escaped the meaning it gave them. Blackmur's

play with "real" and "actual" and their variations carries us away, finally, from rhetoric toward the territory of pure expressionist poetry.

6. *The Mystical Rhetoric of Negation.* This final rhetorical category to be considered here should be regarded as transitional—like Blackmur's dialectic of real and actual—between the rhetoric and the poetry of New Criticism. The rhetoric of negation is, in fact, a language of true mysticism—of Zen, for example. To summarize from a study by Charles Morris, the mystic's attempt to translate his immediate experience into intersubjective terms encounters certain difficulties arising from the disparity between the regular nature of ordinary language and the irregular nature of mystical experience and what Morris calls its spontaneously resulting "primary" language. Because the "complex network of symbolic processes which he is attempting to translate included contradictions," the explainer-mystic finally "resorts to negations." His subject is "nameless, . . . neither temporal nor non-temporal, neither conscious nor non-conscious, neither this nor that." The mystic, frustrated by the communicative difficulties, Morris says, will in the end return to his primary language.[32]

For our immediate purposes here we can make a rough parallel between the poem or art work and the mystic's primary language, and between the remarks of the romantic critic and the mystic's secondary language. Here, for example, is Mrs. Langer advancing a theory of art

(I have italicized the negatives): "The basic concept is the articulate *but non-discursive* form having import *without conventional reference*, and therefore presenting itself *not as a symbol in the ordinary sense*, but as 'significant form,' in which the factor of significance is *not logically discriminated*, but is felt as a quality *rather than recognized as a function*." [33] Even Karl Shapiro once admitted that, like a mystic, he was more willing to say what a poem is not than what it is: "I think of a poem as a literary construct composed of *not-words* which *in their flight from meanings* arrive at a prosodic *sense-beyond-sense*. Its aim *is not known*." [34]

These two very striking examples—one unconscious, one conscious—of the mystical rhetoric of negation should call to mind innumerable more casual, perhaps even gratuitous instances of it located closer to the center of the New Criticism. Perhaps one thinks most naturally of those fretful attempts, like Tate's, to say that poetry provides a unique knowledge: "It is a kind of knowledge *that we did not possess before*. It is *not knowledge 'about'* something else; the poem is the fullness of that knowledge. We know the particular poem, *not what it says* that we can restate. In a manner of speaking, the poem is its own knower, *neither poet nor reader knowing anything that the poem says apart from* the words of the poem." [35] Or even of whole essays in negation, like Brooks' on "The Heresy of Paraphrase." In order to enforce the heresy, he has to proclaim the poem to be a uniquely complex phenomenon of language not translatable, therefore, into common prose. Here is Brooks on the soul of a poem, the "essential structure of a poem (*as distinguished from,*" he writes, "the rational or logical structure of the 'statement' which we abstract from it)": [36]

The principle [of unity] *is not one which involves* the arrangement of the various elements into homogeneous groupings, pairing like with like. It unites the like with the unlike. It *does not unite them,* however, by the simple process of allowing one connotation to cancel out another *nor does it reduce the contradictory attitudes* to harmony by a process of subtraction. The unity *is not a unity* of the sort to be achieved by the reduction and simplification appropriate to an algebraic formula. It is a positive unity, *not a negative;* it represents *not a residue* but an achieved harmony.[37]

Both Tate and Brooks, like Shapiro, have the mystic's usual difficulty in finding intersubjective positives in which to describe their essential experience of or belief about the nature of poetry. The best they can produce is vague and inadequate abstraction, or else citations of what they regard as illuminating analogies—as Brooks cites architecture, ballet, and music [38]—which last recourse, perhaps, like Tate's trope of the poem as its own knower, is a gesture of return toward the mystic's "primary" language of his immediate experience of essences. The integral relation of mysticism, so far as it is evidenced in these New Critical examples of the rhetoric of negation, to what we call romanticism I count as too well agreed upon to need elaborate additional pointing up here.

POETIC CUNNING AND THE INDUCTION OF PIETIES

The dividing line between the rhetoric and the poetry of the New Criticism, it will already be clear, is no very definite one. But I think there is usefulness in recognizing at least this much of a distinction: that the rhetoric of the New Criticism—the persuasive maneuvers closer to the language of speculative philosophers than to the language of poets—functions on the whole to restrict and discourage in advance doubt and argument of a logical or empirical sort, so that actually positive creation of attitudes and beliefs about the nature of poetry can be undertaken by the more magical powers of the critics as virtual poets. We turn now to some instances of that poetic cunning, and first to the feelings and attitudes that it functions to create and sustain in behalf of a New Critical mystique of poetry.

1. *The Poetries of Love and Dread.* I think it can be said with at least approximate truth that among New Critics Ransom is the critic-poet of love and sentiment, and Blackmur the critic-poet of dread and passion. The two poets are complementary examples of the same religious or religious-like experience in its two possible visions—the pietistic and the Dionysiac.

Ransom's, of course, is a cheerful sort of pietism.

Nature is innocent, beautiful, to be loved, in the simple way that God loved the world as He made it, or that Jesus loved the children, or St. Francis the birds. Innocence, holiness, love—these are also the values that motivate the performance of religious observances, and that inhabit the work of art. "The aesthetic moment," he writes in *The World's Body*, "appears as a curious moment of suspension; between the Platonism in us, which is militant, always sciencing and devouring, and a starved inhibited aspiration towards innocence which, if it could only be free, would like to respect and know the object as it might of its own accord reveal itself." [39] Art as a gesture of innocent and contemplative love for some instance of nature "for its own sake" is, then, at once a beloved object in itself and an icon of a beloved object. Nature perceived in such innocence and love becomes animate, and the "uses" to which man puts it without reverence, love, aesthetic joy, come to be seen in terms of human atrocities—plunder and rape. Sometimes, as when Ransom challenges "the geometer to define for us the configuration of the pebble," nature is seen pluckily resisting: "The gallant pebble will defy the geometer. . . ." The slightest object, in the end, will defy the most ravenously appetitive mind; for the World's Body—unabstractable, infinitely various thingness-in-itself—"will never submit to determination." [40]

The whole world of Ransom's criticism is inspirited and embodied with life. Everything in his essays, poems

as well as natural objects (Milton's trimeter couplets
in the Nativity hymn "take the stage jauntily, and
speak up clearly, but . . . the long lines are always
waiting to step forward and complete what they have
started"),[41] is ready to speak, move, suffer, love, be; to
assume the shape of life, usually garbed in primal innocence. As a poet of criticism, Ransom has endowed the
world with body. Yet his ingenuous poet-voice, incul-
cating love and reverence for nature, and dallying, in
order to do so, with sentimentality, protects itself and us
from embarrassment by assuming from time to time a
grosser foreign voice—a counter-rhetoric of bombast
and self-mockery ("the gallant pebble"). A most ironic
and intellectual sentimentalist he, in the end, a most
Oxonian innocent.

The poet in Blackmur's prose, in contrast, shines
through in more lurid colors. His is not the innocent
vision, but the fallen vision—perhaps the pagan vision:
the vision darkly but intensely perceived and embraced
with tragically failing desire. Blackmur's is the poet-
voice of the wilder emotions, of dread and passion, a
voice raised to sing in agony of the mysteries, to sum-
mon both a sense of them and a reverence for them.
Here is an extraordinary incantation from "Lord Tennyson's Scissors" on behalf of the deeper meanings—the
"gesture," or the silent voice beyond, or the "song" beneath, the prose-powers of words—of a particular text.
Blackmur quotes from "The Dry Salvages" ("The salt

is on the briar rose, / The fog is in the fir trees"), and this is what he hears and wants to make us hear in those lines:

Here is the salt of death and of truth and of savor, the salt in our souls of that which is not ours, moving there. The salt is on the wild and thorny rose grappling in the granite at sea's edge, grappling and in bloom, almost ever-blooming; and it is the rose which was before, and may yet be after, the rose of the Court of Love, or the rose of the Virgin. It is the rose out of the garden which includes the rose in the garden. There is in Eliot's line (alien but known to our line that we read) also all the roses that have been in his life, as in the next line is all the fog. The fog is another salt as the fir trees are another rose. It is all there is in fog that lowers, covers, silences, imperils, menaces and caresses; but in it, as it is in them; there is the slowed apparition, coming up under an island, of evergreen struggling, tenacious life. The two together make an image, and in their pairing reveal, by self-symbol declare, by verse and position unite, two halves of a tragic gesture.[42]

There is "interpretation" here, of course. But the main function of the passage is to evoke from and for Eliot's text—by the rhythms and repetitions and recurrences of sound, and the combining and opposing of images in obscure relations of implied meaning and modification of meaning, by, in short, techniques of a secondary super-imposed poetry of Blackmur's own—a sense of mysteries intuited and occulted in awe and passion.

Allen Tate is also sometimes an effective poet of dread,

but of a somewhat different order from Blackmur. He, too, has seen the dark vision; but it is monkish rather than pagan or Nietzschean in its coloring—the vision of the dark night of the soul. Where Blackmur, having sipped the honey dew, cleaves to necessity by luxuriating in the dread and rolling with the passion, Tate practices sitting still and seems to close tight ascetic lips over what he feels. When he speaks, his voice, like the voice of the haggard sinner-saint sorely tried and fresh from agonies of rage and pain and temptation, most characteristically gives the impression of great interior intensities suppressed. The result, often, is a prose-poetry of beautifully modulated dourness, a voice of scarred endurance and suppressed hysteria that moves by saying so much less than is felt and known. It is a voice that involves us in the special dread and passion of sin and salvation.

In the earlier essay on Hart Crane, for example, one literally "hears" the iron restraint of understatement, the effect in the opening pages of bleak disorder in the fragmented and discontinuous progress of the paragraphs as antiphonally arranged (one biographical, then one literary), and the tone throughout of dulled and stolid grief. These are the poetic instruments by which Tate *creates* an immediate felt sense, outside the "meaning" of the essay, of grief, of waste, of the actual disorder of both Crane's life and the age that bred him.[43] There are a number of more local examples in Tate's essays of this almost incantatory, almost liturgical technique. In "Techniques of Fiction," for one, Tate is suggesting at one point that in a particular sense Flaubert "created" modern fiction. "And I do not like to think that Flaubert created modern fiction," Tate writes, "because I do not like Flaubert." But then it occurs to him that Stendhal provided Flaubert with his essential artistic inheritance. Again he intones: "I do not like to think that Stendhal did this because I do not like Stendhal." [44] The effect of this incidental passage (he means he "does not like," or recoils from, their barbarian manners) in an essay on the workings of imagination in fiction, is to flash forth suddenly a gratuitous instance, bred by the accidents of the immediate context, of Tate's continuing sense of anger and despair at the dislocation of traditional human values in the modern world. It is an instance of Tate's "voice" —the squeak of pain or madness swallowed and held down—an instance of the sustaining poetic vehicle that makes his work one and that carries so well the burden of his particular themes.

2. *The Poetries of Fleeting Insight.* The poetries we have just left create, in their different ways, feelings of what some reality is like beyond, below, or above the cognitive abilities of our everyday brute natures. Each creates, perhaps largely by means of persistence of tone, its own aura of things "far more deeply interfused" than such ordinary constituents of life as the prose meanings, say, of our everyday discourse, or our casual,

running experiences of everyday nature. These deeper things, these knowledges, these mysteries, even, are the stuff of insight or revelation, poking up only occasionally, and then perhaps blindingly or paralyzingly, into the world of consciousness. This is why the critics often, if not always, speak as poets. For poets are, after all, the traditional bearers of those moments of insight and truth. So there is an implict secondary poetry, encompassing and protecting the primary poetry characterized in the preceding section, whose special purpose is to say, "I have just had an inrush of truth, and I am giving it to you as best I can in my poor way. If I think about it I may lose it altogether in the hard cold mazes of rational care. And besides I must keep ready and open for more possible inrushes; let the head come up just long enough for a gulp of the thin intellectual air, but it must then be drowned again as quickly as possible in the dark, warm, trembling depths of the heart. The final, full, finished wisdom will come late, if it ever comes at all. Now I am just a humble receptacle, an occasional halting voice."

So Ransom's essays in *The World's Body* are "preparations for criticism," [45] and Blackmur thinks criticism is "the formal discourse of an amateur" (with the added French intent).[46] And Tate, on a recent collection of his essays—"I am not sure that I wanted to write more than three or four of these essays; the others I was asked to write; one can do what one does. I never knew what I thought about anything until I had written about it. To write an essay was to find out what I thought; for I did not know at the beginning how or where it would end." [47]

Thus, too, the tentativeness, or vagueness, or the outright playfulness of so many of the titles, which are another part of this secondary protective poetry. They are a sign of the editor who has come knocking into the critic-poet's dream or meditation to ask him what at the moment he is thinking. Aroused, the critic-poet does what he can till the dream comes down again. He puts forth "Causeries," "Queries," "Emphases," "Thoughts on," "Preliminary Notes," and numberless "Notes" on or toward—Notes not in the scholar's sense, but in the sense of spontaneous and isolated first thoughts. And often the critic will pause midway in his thoughts ingenuously to confess some bafflement or ignorance: "Perhaps the last sentence brings me to my topic; I am not quite sure." (Ransom).[48] "Suppose you feel, as I do, that after Rawdon Crawley comes home (I believe from jail—it is hard to remember Thackeray)" . . . (Tate).[49] This is largely a matter of tone, of course, particularly the familiar reluctance of the critic to go to the bookshelf and check his source ("Coleridge says somewhere . . .")—a tone rhetorically expressive, often, of imperatives against "scientism" and "methodology" in all forms, and their dangers for the aliveness of intelligence and sensibility.

All this adds up to a sentimental sub-poetry, in the New Criticism, of the ultimate failure of intellectual certainty. Sometimes, as in Tate and Blackmur, we find poetries actually in celebration of ignorance. For example, this passage on Adams from Blackmur's "The Expense of Greatness":

The greatness of the mind of Adams . . . is in the acceptance, with all piety, of ignorance as the humbled form of knowledge; in the pursuit of divers shapes of knowledge—the scientific, the religious, the political, the social and trivial—to the point where they add to ignorance, when the best response is silence itself. That is the greatness of Adams as a type of mind. As it is a condition of life to die, it is a condition of thought, in the end, to fail. Death is the expense of life and failure is the expense of greatness.[50]

The effect of these incidental poetries of fleeting insight and ultimate ignorance is to sustain pieties in behalf of mystery, with such pieties working to free the critic for unlimited excursionings of feeling and speculation at the same time that they surround and cut off the reasoner and scientist as heretics of intellectual pride.

3. *The Critic as Tragic Hero.* Having glanced at some of his lyric forms, we turn now—with the Blackmuresque echo still in the air—to the great form, the underlying Master Trope of the romantic New Critic. There has been a preoccupation in the writings of New Critics—most vividly in Blackmur and Tate—with the replacement of the traditional hero by the artist himself

as the special expression in literature of modern cultural decay in general. I should like to propose a tentative extension of this very interesting perception into the area of literary criticism. If in some real sense modern criticism has tended to become poetry, and if the artist has in fact sometimes tended to become the hero— usually tragic—of his own dramatic creations, then the conception of the critic as tragic hero is at least not hopelessly fanciful.

Alfred Kazin once felt irritated with the New Critics' tone of "pride in a private greatness and private spiritual tragedy." [51] Though one need not necessarily subscribe to the particular cultural liberalism from which his irritation with aesthetic critics proceeded, I think it is easy enough to see a certain truth in Kazin's observation. Here is Blackmur, for example, on the dangerous temptations of virtuoso criticism, criticism that becomes a habit of mind, a consuming art, a self-sufficient vision, even a way of life: "It becomes, as we say, unconscious, so crowded it is with intuition, and cries in the dark, crowding its darkness into the blaze of noon. Then it becomes pure criticism of pure literature: pure heroism in a world without heroes, pure expression without reflection." [52] Though the last phrase somewhat qualifies the force of what goes before it, Blackmur is suggesting a kind of damnation awaiting the critic who loses sight of the object of his criticism, whose processes of criticism become their own ends. We are reminded of Tate's vision of Poe as God: intellection without an object. But to come closer to the reality of the critic as such, the Poe analogy may be translated into the threat of criticism "for its own sake"—or criticism-as-poetry— where criticism seems to absorb, even *become*, the object which created it and for which it exists as a dependent.

Blackmur knows the dangers here. But he knows them almost too vividly, too intimately. He says that "moral philosophy," implying also religion, is necessary to "save" such criticism. Is Blackmur not often his own tragic hero, unsaved, bending to the force of his own trope? Tate gives the tragedy a full stage at the end of "Is Literary Criticism Possible?," where the hazardous but necessary relation of critic to poem is seen in cosmic terms:

Literary criticism, like the Kingdom of God on earth, is perpetually necessary and, in the very nature of its middle position between imagination and philosophy, perpetually impossible. . . . It is the nature of man and of criticism to occupy the intolerable position. Like man's, the intolerable position of criticism has its own glory.[53]

This is Christian, Dantesque tragedy. The tragedy is the tragedy of the imagination, of straining but limited vision. The critic, like Dante in his dream, has about him the implications of tragedy in that he cannot wholly attain—for all his yearnings and his pieties—to the Beatific Vision of the poem in the prose-life of his criticism. The poem, the critics tell us again and again, is

ultimately untranslatable, unanalyzable: "No observation, no collection of observations, ever tells the whole
story; there is always room for more, and at the hypo-
thetical limit of attention and interest there will always
remain, quite untouched, the thing itself" (Blackmur).[54]
It is only another step to this observation by Vivas in
the essay "What Is a Poem?," which provides, in spite
of the grossness of the vehicular image, a clear statement
of the constituents of the critic as tragic hero, the critic
as representative man embodying, as it were, the essentials of the human condition seen as aspiration and
failure: "Were we able," he writes, "to put our cognitive
teeth on the aorta of Being itself, and were we able to
drink the truth directly from it, were we not forced to
approach Being humbly, through the mediation of symbols, we would see the world as God sees it." [55]

POETIC CUNNING AND THE CREATION OF EXEMPLARY
IMAGES OF THE NATURE OF POETRY

So far the critics have induced awarenesses of mystery,
and along with them the appropriate pieties; they have
created the poetry of themselves as dreamers, metaphysical sufferers, and contemplatives awaiting the influxions
of spirit; and we have had evoked in behalf of the critic
the tragic potentials of fear and pity, even of glory. We
are now prepared to observe the final creative act of our
critic-poets, the act or complex of acts for which the

others we have discussed are but preparations: the creation of images of the nature of poetry. This, we shall see, involves the poetic imagining of a whole religion of poetry, complete with worshippers, images and holy objects, and a corps of spiritual fathers.

1. *Approach as Supplicative Ritual.* Vivas' use above of the word "approach" in a context of yearning for God's vision of Being, suggests, in perspective with the virtually religious value poetry seems to have for the critics, that the word has a rather special felt significance. It is a familiar word in criticism, especially in the New Critics' meditations about what they and other critics do or are about to do with a poem. Critics try one approach, fail with it, try another. They argue over one another's approaches. Most deny the wisdom of sticking to one approach. And some, like Blackmur, positively preach the necessity of an endlessly changing multiplicity of approaches: "In making a formal approach to Marianne Moore," for example, one must worry preliminarily over "special terms and special adjustments;" [56] and "the later poetry of William Butler Yeats is certainly great enough . . . to warrant a special approach, deliberately not the only approach, and deliberately not a complete approach." [57] Tate's imagining, in one essay, the critical approach as a military action ("you have got to do a little here and a little there, and you may not be of the command that enters the suburbs of Berlin") [58] is not without precedent in religious poetry ("Better my heart, three-personed God. . . ."),

and seems to confirm by a freshening image the feeling that the critical "approach" is rather like the religious footwork of supplicative ritual.

I am suggesting that the recurring jargon about critical approaches, with their dangers and insufficiencies and provisionalities, seems to imagine—under pressure from the religious moods we have been discovering in the New Criticism—that the critic is some sort of supplicant approaching in a reverence of hesitation some sort of deity. Poetry, as we have seen, is ultimately ineffable; one cannot consummate and possess, for poetry, though a fountainhead of knowledges, is itself a mystery. And individual poems—like Yeats' "The Apparitions" as seen by Blackmur—may sometimes display the arbitrariness and protean recalcitrance of the demon or god; [59] some gods prefer fresh-killed heifer, some prefer flowers, and some, without reason, will prefer heifer one day and flowers another. So the relation of the critic to the poem emerges dramatistically as that of devout to oracle or spirit: he makes his supplicative, his elicitative approaches, receives blinding illumination or partial insight—or perhaps only rebuff, which will require him to retreat and try another approach. Surely this amounts also to a clarification, in more specific imagery, of the potentials of the modern critic as tragic hero.

2. *The Iconography of the Poem as Creature and of Poetry as Deity:* The poem as mysterious or occult object becomes surrounded with icons that both remind reverence and body forth intimations or approximations

of its nature. Because it is regarded as organic, even as an essence, and therefore inexhaustible by the machineries of mechanical description, the poem is understood perhaps initially in animate terms, then more specially in images of ourselves, which are in turn images, though corrupt and approximate, of God. Thus it may be seen as gestating: "The genuine work of art comes from the unknown depths of the soul, where its growth is even more mysterious than the development of a foetus" (Vivas).[60] As acquiring the pronouns of personality: "The word poetry has crept in here unannounced, and needs to be qualified lest he become a usurper, or worse a restored monarch." (Blackmur).[61] As desiring: " 'Poetry' . . . is words which are free to mean as they please (which need not be 'as you or I please')" (Richards).[62] As reasoning and choosing: "Poetry wants to be pure, but poems do not. At least, most of them do not want to be too pure. The poems want to give us poetry. . . ." (Robert Penn Warren).[63] And, as a consequence of their choices, achieving a rank and quality as "higher" or "lower," "more powerful" or "less powerful," approximately in the manner of saints going to heaven and getting their appropriate rewards and recognitions: "The souls that form the great rose of Paradise are seated in banks and tiers of ascending blessedness, but they are all saved, they are all perfectly happy; they are all 'pure,' for they have all been purged of mortal taint." [64]

These final cheering images of Warren's carry us to-

ward a transitional proposition: as the nature of the individual *Poem* tends to be imaginatively understood by
the critics in terms of the iconography either of man as
divine but impurely divine creature or of Christ as pure
Deity incarnate in the impurities of creature, so the
nature of the species *Poetry* tends to be understood in
terms of the iconography of pure Deity, or Being. Thus
the association with poetry of the idea of "salvation" and
its preliminaries of repentance and atonement: "There
is a hybris of science for which science has no way of
atoning; for it denies poetry which could alone become
its conscience" (Fiedler).[65] And the supporting sacramental imagery: Tate affirms that "works of literature
. . . are the recurrent discovery of the human communion"; [66] and Blackmur, in "Toward a Modus
Vivendi," echoing Eliot's trope of poetry's "making
the Word flesh," [67] gives "the Word" (humane letters)
the weight of a possible counter-evangelism to the
increasingly universal dissemination of minimal mass
culture in the modern world.[68] "All proximate incarnations of the Word," Tate observes in "The Symbolic
Imagination," reflecting on Saint Catherine's miracu-
lously smelling the blood of Christ, "are shocking,
whether in Christ and the Saints, or in Dostoevsky,
James Joyce, or Henry James." [69]

3. *The Shepherds and the Fathers of the Church:* If
the Poem is to be imagined as either Host or revealed
Word in a relation of descent from or incarnation of

the overarching spirit that is Poetry, it is natural that upon occasion the critics should imagine themselves as custodial priests or sustaining Church Fathers. Robert Gorham Davis once sketched out in a perceptive essay some of the parallels, as the New Critics treated it, between the poem and traditional orthodoxy.[70] Alfred Kazin once charged the critics with being "talmudists." [71] And a more recent commentator has grumbled that "if there's all this *mana* in the content (or is it the form?) of literature, it's easy to see how, if not why, the critic soon becomes not only schoolmaster but also priest." [72] Exactly. And so in a *Kenyon* of a few years ago one finds Ransom as parson preaching a little sermon on the "trinitarian existence" of the Poem, quaintly drawing his exempla from the Eden story and Plato's construct of the Forms; "the meters" are as the beads of prayer, the signs of ideal and changeless order, by which we implicitly beseech the Platonic heaven for deliverance from death: "In our verse perhaps more frequently than we know," he muses, "we are calling down the blessings of Heaven." [73] Or R. P. Blackmur preaching a grand cathedral address upon the mysteries of Numen and Moha—his text, "'I' have seen what I have seen, see what I see," and his emblematic pageant (he modestly calls it "a kind of critical poem imitating the behavior of the mind") engaging the personified services of Myth, Historia, Lore, Fortuna, Filosophia, Scientia, and, of course, Poetry.[74] And Blackmur states his belief, in "A

Burden for Critics," that one has to treat poetry critically
as the church fathers treated the canon of scripture.
"We have to make plain," Blackmur insists, "not only
what people are reading, but also—as Augustine and the
other fathers had to do with the scriptures—what they
are reading about." [75] At the end of the same essay he
brings us back to the trope of the Poem as divine creature when he writes that the "ideal" critical judgment is
"theological": "as a soul is judged finally, quite apart
from its history, for what it really is at the moment of
judgment." [76]

OBSERVATIONS ON CRITICISM AS POETRY

  Blackmur's sounding the note of judgment above invites evaluative thoughts about the rhetoric and poetry
of the New Criticism we have been sampling here.
Poetry-as-knowledge, it seems, breeds criticism-as-
poetry—criticism that is less strenuously exegetical and
analytical than it is expressive and evocative. Because
we have been jocularly aware, since the appearance of
Stanley Edgar Hyman's *The Armed Vision*, of the
"criticism of criticism" as a virtual sub-literary genre,
perhaps we may be justified in assuming momentarily
within the sub-genre a more intricately decadent and
parasitic specialization of it: the criticism of criticism-
as-poetry. One commentator, in a published appreciation
of Ransom's critical work, actually set us a precedent a

few years ago in *Western Review* upon which to found such an assumption. For he saw Ransom's criticism, like the poem that Ransom's criticism sees, as a kind of beloved object, perhaps ultimately irreducible, untranslatable, inexhaustible: "The benefits that are potential in it," he wrote with the humility of the critic of criticism-as-poetry, "will be elicited not by the act of praise, but only by discovering the object as in itself it really is." [77]

But the fact is that not all observers are pleased with criticism as poetry. Louis Grudin, for example, incensed by the relatively mild literariness of Eliot's essays, once went so far as to coin a searingly deprecatory name—"literary crypticism"—for what results from "the attempt to write criticism with the means and motives which operate in the writing of poetry." [78] And both the general distress over Blackmur and the occasional growls in the direction of usually less elaborate stylists like Tate ("scrubby ecstasy," "blood-and-thunder language of sin and salvation") [79] are well known.

There have even been objections from within the ranks to intrusions of "personality" into the critical labor. Cleanth Brooks, a New Critic whose style has always been efficient and spare, and who—aside from a catchword or two—has contributed nothing to the poetry of New Criticism, once defended to Alfred Kazin the supposed "impersonality" of the New Critic (a supposition not easily supported outside Brooks' own work) and indicated his opposition to criticism that attempts "rivalry with the work of art." [80] Tate, who likes to remind his readers that he is writing *essays* in the traditional sense, and thus leaves room for a degree of both looseness in the method and literary grace in the writing, nevertheless stresses that he writes "opinion, and neither aesthetics nor poetry in prose;" "critical style," he declares in the preface to *On the Limits of Poetry*, "ought to be as plain as the nose on one's face; . . . it ought not to compete in the detail of sensibility with the work which it is privileged to report on." [81] Even Blackmur has insisted that the critic is simply a maker of connecting bridges so that perception and understanding can pass more easily between writer and reader,[82] or at most a "go-between," a discrete, disappearing Pandarus of the arts.[83] Only Ransom, among the critics, comes forth bravely in defense of the critic as something of a poet, congratulating Tate on teaching "creative writing" so that it may include criticism, alluding to Arnold's authoritative belief that criticism exercises "the creative intelligence," [84] savoring Eliot's critical prose because it "has some of the value of literature." [85] Ransom disparages the "schoolmaster" critic, like Aristotle, because art invites an art response, a secondary poetic frenzy, which the schoolmaster suppresses. He prefers the critic who, as he says in his essay on Aristotle, starts ideally "with a spontaneous surge of piety, and is inducted by the contagion of art into a composition of his own, which sustains the warmth unashamed, and probably manages a rounded literary effect, having a beginning, a middle, and an end." [86]

But whatever one's side in the stylistic argument, there is no room for dispute about the fact that the New Critics have characteristically chosen strongly rhetorical, even poetical manners of addressing the world, and that, in spite of some considerable leeway for stylistic individuality, they have formed those manners in the image of a quasi-religion of poetry. The nature of poetry is of course what all criticism and theory, whether implicitly or explicitly, is in the end "about." Poetry is important because of its peculiar "nature." A poem is good or bad according to the aptness of its realization of poetry's "nature." Though such statements usually may be discerned as describing a perfectly empty logical circle, their very circularity urges the psychological fact that beliefs about poetry and acts of criticism of a poem are inseparable in the New Criticism, as in any other. Though no one would seriously propose that the New Critics "really" believe that literature is revelation, or that poetry is divinity, or that critics are priests and theologians, the sensibility for such beliefs is there. Where there is so much myth-making and magical perceiving going on, the appropriate feeling, the sensibility, must be present too. And if "sensibility" may be defined as something like the aesthetic or substantive organ of belief, we can see that a romantic version of religious sensibility is present in the writings of most

New Critics, working itself into patterns and images that create—in ironic opposition to the abstractions of orthodox and traditional thought and faith that the critics intellectually accept—the *likeness* or *experience* of such beliefs.

W. K. Wimsatt, Jr., who is both a Catholic and a scholar-New Critic, observed in *The Verbal Icon* that "the vocabulary and main assumptions of recent criticism have been developing in a way that makes it now difficult to speak well of poetry without participating in a joint defense of poetry and religion, or at least without a considerable involvement in theology." [87] This remark seems to miss the point of its author's own dissatisfaction with "quasi-religious" substitutes—particularly substitutes of poetry—for the real thing in the modern world. "Recent criticism"—by which he means, for the most part, New Criticism—in its simultaneous defense both of poetry and of orthodoxy and tradition has been making paradoxical gestures of self-annihilation. The very passion of its defense has bred chimeric images and visions, even diabolical arguments, a seductive rhetoric and poetry of critical discourse, in short, that would seem to lure us in a hellish direction—toward the virtual heresies, born of romantic enthusiasms, of a religion of poetry.

PART IV

The Importance of the New Criticism

A good work of criticism is a work of art about another work of art.

KARL SHAPIRO

chapter 9

Literature and the Literary Essay

"ONE looks in vain through the writings of subtle and 'philosophical' minds like I. A. Richards, William Empson, Kenneth Burke, and the younger men who have adopted their terminology," Henri Peyre complained several years ago, "for *one* excellent article of criticism." [1] Of course, anyone even a little conversant with the writings of these men (who, by the way, are the "younger men" that have been searched through "in vain"?) would feel unhappy at Professor Peyre's having allowed his irritability to make him appear ignorant. But for the critic himself, or the student of criticism, the professor's statement would have other echoes of interest. It would recall, first of all, the whole ethos of the contemporary critics' assault upon the institutionalized inertia of mind and imagination characteristic, until recent years, of the study of literature in the universities.

But more important, it introduces two words, "excellent" and "criticism," which symbolize perhaps the most vitally strategic ideas in the former war between the Professors and the Critics, and which, even now, any critic or critic-of-critics has to be responsible for making clear to himself.

But whatever "good" or "excellent" criticism may finally be, I think it is striking how frequently and consistently the New Critics and their associates have been blamed or praised for doing things essentially unrelated to criticism, things *non*critical or *other than* critical—at least if we hang on to a fairly common-sense idea of what literary criticism is. Isn't this at the heart of Professor Peyre's complaint when he puts "philosophical" into a little scoff of quotation marks? Stanley Edgar Hyman once charged, a charge variously echoed by other commentators, that Ransom, Tate, and others who produced "manifestoes" in behalf of "close technical reading of texts" failed, on the whole, to practice their own preachments.[2] This was the point of Harry Levin's objection many years ago to Blackmur's proliferating mannerisms ("a fondness for onomatopoetic suggestion, a deliberate cultivation of the malapropism, a tendency to fall victim to his own metaphors; epigrams that fizzle, paradoxes that turn out to be mere contradictions, desperate efforts to achieve a platitude"[3]), all of which were signs of a flourishing self-consciousness that was essentially irrelevant to the business-like pursuit of criticism. But Robert W. Stallman, in contrast, certainly implied no disapproval in describing Ransom as "primarily a philosopher . . . only incidentally committed to the technical criticism of poetry." [4] And more recently Professor Hugh Holman implied praise when he described Ransom as having "fostered and practiced a criticism that is philosophically oriented," and Tate as having a "sharply logical and profoundly philosophical mind." [5]

So it appears that at least in some eyes the critics are up to something that is much of the time other than criticism, if criticism, reduced to the lowest common denominator of probable agreement on its meaning, denotes the analysis and evaluation of literary works. This other than critical something—an irrelevancy or an enrichment, depending on your viewpoint—would seem to range somewhere between general philosophy (Hyman, for example, praises Empson and the early Blackmur for examining texts while the other critics are preoccupied with "general critical problems, some of them remote from literature" [6]) and self-realization (John Edward Hardy praises the "plain, steady, utilitarian" manner of Cleanth Brooks as an antidote to the dangers of "inspired" criticism).[7] The intent realized in Brooks' critical style as described by Hardy would be a rather far cry from Ransom's notion that the critic ought to write literarily. The "plain, steady, utilitarian" style would be close, I would judge, to the "schoolmaster's" style. Certainly it would not easily fit Leslie Fiedler's conception of the "true" language of criticism as "the language of conversation—the voice of the dilettante at home." [8] Among the major New Critics, only Cleanth Brooks comes to mind—and perhaps also Empson—as engaging mainly in the detailed and selfless analysis of particular works of literature, even though these analyses may also serve as examples in support of theory. With the exception of a few brief analytical "notes" from Tate, of Blackmur's earlier textual studies of certain poets, of an occasional illustrative passage from Richards and a few special items like Ransom's study of Shakespeare's language and Tate's detailed discussion of his own "Ode," we have mostly general or "speculative" essays from the critics. In the manner of the essayist, the critics, even when they begin with a text or a corpus of texts, will tend to move away toward general considerations of the imagination, the modern world, the nature of poetry, even the nature of reality. As a consequence of such subjects and intentions, "style," as the expression of the necessarily personal mood of reflection or speculation, assumes the importance of individuality. Thus the effect of "personality" being realized in or obtruded into so much of the work of the New Critics.

There is a certain paradox—which makes a fine point of attack for the opposition—in this fact of the New Critics, who, after all, hounded the age back to the text and the conscious analytical reading of it, giving so much of their energies to writing "literary essays," essays on the whole *un*analytical and often not unlike, perhaps, the literary "impressionism" they once resisted. But of course not all literary impressionism is of the same value. Assuming the practical worth of impersonal textual and technical analysis, the sort of thing done so well by Brooks and by the many inheritors of his skills who write for the literary magazines and the best academic journals, I should like to explore possibilities for the defense of the other voice of the New Criticism. Call it the "personal," the "impressionistic," the "speculative" voice, as distinguished from the "impersonal" or "analytical" voice. It is the voice that throughout this study has been shown constantly to betray the critics' shared sensibility as a romantic one, the voice of "criticism-as-poetry." Because the inadequacies of the critical positions represented by the old-fashioned academician and the journalist-reviewers make one wary of seeming to abet their causes in any way, it seems both fitting and necessary to consider fully the available virtues of this "criticism-as-poetry"—or, to neutralize the term, the "literary essay" as it has been variously practiced by the New Critics.

An obvious defense might be derived from the New Critics' doctrines against "scientism" and the anti-humane worship of method. The literary essay, by its very looseness and tentativeness, tends, perhaps, to keep the mind liberal, free, responsive, and thus preserves it from the habits of what Eliseo Vivas calls "methodolatry."

But there are other possible important defenses, based on what such essays have actually accomplished. I. A. Richards, who has really done so little as a practical critic (and very little more, though he has *written* a lot, as a "theorist"), has almost singlehandedly motivated the modern critical revolution by haranguing against modern man's educated inabilities to read and understand. And, again almost singlehandedly, he has institutionalized the key concepts of the revolution—"Imagination," the complexity of language's "meaning" as experience, and the bogey of "stock response," which fathered psychologistically the New Critics' descriptions of good poetry in terms of "irony," "paradox," "tension," "impurity"— largely through the pure fervor of his wonder at the ways of words. Because he was perhaps the first to see both what was wrong and what was needed, he deserves the recognition he now has—along with Eliot, the great rediscoverer of the literature of the past in terms of contemporary sensibility—as an established classic of modern criticism.

There have been a great many gestures toward theory among critics following Richards, some pretty systematic, like those of Wimsatt, Wellek and Warren, and the allied aestheticians, but most of them more casual and essayistic—by Tate, Penn Warren, Brooks, Blackmur, and Ransom, to name only the major people. These excursions into theory have been made usually for the purpose of coming back with some definition of the nature of poetry, or of good poetry, and of its importance to us. And most of them have yielded what Richards likes to call "speculative instruments"—that is, metaphors or catchwords by which to conceive or "see," or to inquire further into, the nature of poetry. Of all the New and related critics who have gone in pursuit of theory, it seems to me that John Crowe Ransom has had the largest and best success. In his whole critical life work he has devoted himself to only two or three major ideas, running them through and through his essays, refining them and perfecting them into, as I believe, the truest speculative instruments of this kind that we have had from any of the critics, including Richards, or Coleridge via Richards. The key virtue of Ransom's achievement is that he has taken the pains to give us not a mere clever tag, but an *idea*. For in the trope of the texture-structure dichotomy and its refinement into the idea of the Concrete Universal, Ransom, by identifying the special nature of poetry with the experienced concretions' relation of abundant excess to the rational meaning, has made a definition both of poetry and its psychological reception by a proper reader. The poem has more detail than the meaning requires. And *because* of this we *care* for the poem beyond its use as "meaning." This is what all the critics have always been saying, of course, even those who have protested Ransom's "inorganic" theory. But none has said it so clearly or so well. And in these days when the reigning ambition is to huddle all the arts indiscriminately together under one great universal formula, Ransom's theory has the additional value—his own belief to the contrary—of being formulated so as to fit verbal art best if not exclusively. Taking for granted the indisputable grace and wit of his essays as essays, I think a sound defense of Ransom as a literary essayist could be made, then, on the grounds of his having constructed with such care and sensitivity a particularly effective theoretical idea or metaphor, a useful speculative—or persuasive or pedagogical—instrument for the examination and defense of poetry in a world where such instruments and defenses are peculiarly necessary.

Tate has been spoken of almost as often as Ransom as a "philosopher" among New Critics. But I think that his essays, seen as a whole, are closer to Eliot than to the theoretical pursuits of Richards and Ransom. One always feels the personality in Eliot's essays. It has its formal public face on, but behind that face is a living sensibility, a cultivated intelligence that eschews "method" and records its awarenesses and judgments pretty immediately. In Tate's essays the personality is more vivid, less formal—at least it seems so much less formal that the essays as a body take on the immediacy and drama almost of the confessional. As Tate himself very well realizes and, if we may believe his prefaces, intends, the essays are the record of the progress of a mind. The overpowering sincerity of Tate's essays, even the ingenuousness of their occasional vanities and posturings, make something very special of them. Most of them cannot quite be called criticism. But they are something rarer, richer in substance finally than "pure" criticism— like Ransom's essays, they are literature themselves: they are the biography of the conscience and sensibility of a deeply responsive and complicated man of letters in a peculiarly troubled time. And as that they create part of the myth of our time. Sometimes, in addition, they discover special and unforeseen responses to certain familiar writers—to Poe particularly, but also to Dante, Emily Dickinson, Dostoievski, and of course to Tate himself—that change one's own perception of them for good. They are always handsomely written, too. All this, it seems to me, makes them not only defensible, but indispensable.

Blackmur's criticism is also remarkable for the power, found occasionally in Tate, of creating or recreating one's mode of perception of some work or works. It is in fact *the* characteristic, understood as more vivid and radical in Blackmur's work than in Tate's, and as increased to many more instances, that I shall make the principal basis for arguing that Blackmur is the most important of the New Critics under discussion. Blackmur's peculiar talent has been not merely for analysis or exegesis of texts, but for actually readying in the reader special variations of sensibility necessary for special understanding. As we have seen, Blackmur's earlier style, while never so direct and utilitarian as Brooks', was simpler than the later style about in proportion to his then stricter attention to specific texts. But even his earlier criticism in its final intentions, was quite a different thing from "analysis." Though the earlier essays are full of the analytical work of explaining meanings and scrutinizing the effects of certain technical features of the poem, Blackmur always made these procedures subordinate steps toward the end of creating a mode of perceiving the special quality and receiving the special experience provided in the work of a particular writer. The 1931 essay on Wallace Stevens is a good example. It contrasts Stevens' surface "nonsense" with the meaning*less*ness of Cummings' language and the special compressive techniques of meaning in Pound and Eliot. It then inculcates, by close attention to some "examples" of Wallace Stevens, an understanding of Stevens' particular technique as one of seeing and accumulating ambiguities and pressing them to the point of virtual meaning. This characteristic technique having been isolated, elucidated, and variously exemplified, is thus made available to the reader as a technique of understanding or sensibility, paralleling Stevens' own, with which to surround and possess a poetry whose generalized difficulty is assumed by the critic on behalf of the reader. As in Blackmur's studies of Cummings' diction of sentimental unmeaning, of Marianne Moore's technique of reducing experience by idiosyncrasy and formalism, of

Pound's technique of masks and voices, of Yeats' technique of conception and perception by "magic," this same, more than analytical intention informs most of the earlier essays.

It informs the later essays, too, but its objective there is more complex. In the later essays sensibility is prepared and provided not merely for the appropriate reception of a given, but also for a felt understanding of the disordered time in which we live, of the problems both of artists generally and of particular artists in our time, of what it is that the arts peculiarly "do" with reality, and finally of what essential reality itself is like as immediate unspeakable experience. All these themes may be distinguished, for example, in the long and exotically written essay on Eliot called "Unappeasable and Peregrine." It evokes a sense of our time as deprived of live and valid formative institutions like the Church. It presents the predicament of the artist in such a time in his necessarily makeshift and perhaps chaotic search for the forms and substance in which to create the formal sense of his experience, and delineates Eliot's special act, as a Christian convert, of *realizing* and *recreating* in poetry the substantial experience of the disused form to which he has personally reverted. It demonstrates that art in all times, but particularly in our time of severance from the coherences of the past, is a way of compassing the disorder and flux of experience, of giving it form, of giving us location in it, perhaps even of discovering it for us. And it convinces, finally—accomplishing, like successful art, a suspension of disbelief—that there are depths and mysteries in experience, in "reality," beyond prose and common sense, and graspable only by poetry and imagination. All these subjects are to a degree "talked about" in the Eliot essay; but principally they are evoked, incanted into existence, made intuitively sensible to the reader if he reads successfully. A smaller and more accessible example of Blackmur's performance is this evocation of understanding for Yeats' "The Apparitions":

> One tends to let poems stay too much as they are. Do they not actually change as they are read? Do they not, as we feel them intensely, fairly press for change on their own account? Not all poems, of course, but poems of this character, which engage possibility as *primum mobile* and last locomotive? Is not the precision of the poem for the most part a long way under the precision of the words? Do not the words involve their own opposites, . . . not for contradiction but for development? [9]

These rhetorical questions are not "analysis." But they are part of the almost poetic means by which Blackmur takes the reader into the poem. He also assists the reader to "ad-lib" the poem as Yeats ad-libbed it from the original given iota of insight, and one has the direct experience of how the poem might have gone differently at several junctures. The total effect of all this is to provide an approximate experience of the processes of sensibility with which Yeats himself must have written the poem.

This provision of multiple understandings "from within," so to speak, is the substance not only of the later essays on Yeats and Eliot, but of most of Blackmur's other essays of the forties and fifties. These later essays have a greater sameness about them than the earlier essays, for they all concern themselves with the more general themes of the modern world and the modern artist. But they are also crucially distinct, for each treatment of an individual writer—Mann, James, Dostoievsky, Tolstoy, Flaubert—recreates something of the necessarily individual quality of sensibility needed to grasp the special and different ways each artist had of compassing reality. Mann's "diabolism" is a different thing from Flaubert's exorcising by objective fiction his subjective romantic "demon." Such individuations are certainly an important part of the burden of Blackmur's later efforts as a poet of criticism. For that is what, on the whole, he is—a poet *creating* consciousness, *creating* in his readers a preparatory semblance of the essential experience to come in the poem proper, the experience that, without this readying, might have been missed or violated. Like a poet he *renders* his subjects. Or, as he once said about himself, at the same time denying that his essays "expressed" either himself or a group or institution larger than himself, "I try to express what I am writing about." [10]

We can say very frankly of Blackmur that though his later criticism contains analytical textual examinations, it is in bulk an evocative, insight-giving, impressionistic semi-poetry. Though he can be ludicrous or embarrassing or plain boring, when the frenzy fizzles or when he goes burning on and on without giving light, I believe there is no critic within the New Criticism as it has here been limited that can match him in sensitivity and catholicity and weight of accomplishment. Outside the New Criticism there is only Kenneth Burke, so like him in vitality and reach of imagination and intelligence, so opposite in principle and practice.

Granting Richards and Eliot the unqualified prerogatives of the classic, then, this survey of Ransom as philosopher of literature, of Tate as autobiographer of the man of letters in the modern world, of Blackmur as oracle of the mystiques of poetry and imagination, has been both a sampling of the achievements of the New Critics as literary essayists, and a judgment of those achievements, I think implicitly, as having considerable worth. It has seemed appropriate to make this final positive evaluation in order to head off misinterpretation or misuse of this study by still remaining anti-literary interests. There certainly seem to be more than sufficient grounds on which to assert the importance for our age of the New Criticism. But what I have done in this study is first, in the opening chapter, to proclaim the excellence and magnitude of the achievements of the

New Criticism in recreating the literary sensibility of our time, and then, in succeeding chapters, to set ironic traps for the main proponents of New Criticism so that they may be caught and exposed as romantics. "Romantic" would seem, after all, to be about the worst name one could call a New Critic. It is the name New Critics themselves give to loose art and loose morals, to adversaries who resist religion or imagination, to religionless moralism, to amoral aestheticism, to modern decadence in general. May not the destructive force with which the critics have endowed the word "romantic," when it is turned back upon themselves, seem to threaten annihilation of the value of their causes and achievements?

I think that a defense of the literary essay as a legitimate voice of criticism, a rhetorically supple voice, and a voice that permits itself to range over whatever territory of thought and feeling may be illuminated by the literary work, joins very naturally, in the end, with an at least implicit and partial defense of the romanticism of the New Criticism. All "good" criticism, certainly, must nourish upon "sensibility"—the cultivated but free vision to see according to your living and natural lights what is before you, and from what is given to imagine what is not. This may almost be a description of the poet. And it smacks of the romanticism, the interestingly ironic, the occasionally irritating romanticism of the New Critics.

But what have we as we look toward Chicago and the surviving memorials there of the only other important critical movement of the past twenty years? We have this from Elder Olson: "By 'beauty' I mean the excellence of perceptible form in a composite continuum which is a whole; and by 'excellence of perceptible form' I mean the possession of perceptible magnitude in accordance with a mean determined by the whole as a whole of such-and-such quality, composed of such-and-such parts." [11] And this from Norman Maclean: "The tragedy with depth is compounded out of a profound conception of what is tragic and out of action tragically bent, with characters commensurate to the concept and the act—and, finally, it is composed out of writing." [12] As so often with the Chicagoans, we have the pseudo-philosophic style of the supposed classic color—an imitation of the manner of a bad translation of Aristotle. We have intellectual bathos and circular exterminations of meaning achieved only after the most elephantine laborings of diction and syntax. And these are high points—moments of definition and principle. We have, finally, in the place where sensibility ought to be, huge abstract machineries for the processing, packaging, and labeling of literary produce. But after all the noise and exertion of its construction, the Neo-Aristotelian factory produced hardly anything very memorable—a lively essay or two, at its best, against New Critics—and it now seems to have shut down altogether, though presumably it still stands firm.

It is no doubt significant that most of the major New Critics have been artists as well as critics (Ransom, Tate, Blackmur, Penn Warren, Empson, recently I. A. Richards, and even a poem or two of Brooks' have seen print), and around them have gathered many of the finest younger writers of the time. Sensibility, that agile awareness that for better or for worse dominates the literary essay at the expense of "method," and that in a different dilution is the artist's special medium, is perhaps the chief thing lacking in the work of the Aristotelians and other mechanical critics, including that large majority of academics for whom the chief and lasting legacy of the New Criticism is what they call "explication," or "formalistic analysis." A viableness of sensibility, a readiness for "speculative fury," a susceptibility, at bottom, even to moments of romantic frenzy, these are qualities that gave the New Critics their original impetus to move against the sterility of literary study in their time and to challenge the dehumanizing conditions of the world that bred it. Now that the skills of literary study have been refurbished and revitalized, it may be worth turning back once again to the New Criticism, the chief movement for literary humanism of this century, this time to discover its vision of a humane commitment and belief that can provide for the user of those skills a deepening and liberating idea of their place in the human enterprise at large. We are all necessarily, in this place and time, if we are serious and humane, "romantics" in reaction. The New Critics have created, willy-nilly, by the hard personal labor of their extemporizing a structure of value in the midst of chaos, a major testament of that modern necessity. And perhaps accusations of romantic heresy are a tolerable enough scourge to bear for the privilege of such felicity.

Notes

1. THE IDENTITY OF THE NEW CRITICISM

1. Douglas Bush, "The New Criticism: Some Old-Fashioned Queries," *Publications of the Modern Language Association*, LXIV (March, 1949), 14, 17.

2. Murray Krieger, *The New Apologists for Poetry* (Minneapolis: University of Minnesota Press, 1956), p. 4.

3. T. S. Eliot, "The Frontiers of Criticism," *The Sewanee Review*, LXIV (1956), 525–43.

4. "The New Criticism," A Discussion by William Barrett, Kenneth Burke, Malcolm Cowley, Robert Gorham Davis, Allen Tate, and Hiram Haydn, *The American Scholar*, XX (1950–51), 218.

5. Willard B. Arnold, *The Social Ideas of Allen Tate* (Boston: Bruce Humphreys, 1955), p. 53.

6. Alfred Kazin, *On Native Grounds* (New York: Reynal and Hitchcock, 1942), pp. 429–30.

7. See, for example, Bush, "The New Criticism," pp. 19–20, and Richard H. Fogle, "Romantic Bards and Metaphysical Reviewers, *ELH*, XII (1945), 231.

8. Elder Olson, "William Empson, Contemporary Criticism and Poetic Diction," *Critics and Criticism*, ed. R. S. Crane (Chicago: University of Chicago Press, 1952), p. 45.

9. John Crowe Ransom, "Forms and Citizens," *The World's Body* (New York: Scribner, 1938), p. 42.

10. T. S. Eliot, *Selected Essays* (New York: Harcourt Brace, 1950), pp. 343–54.

11. Allen Tate, "The Man of Letters in the Modern World," *The Man of Letters in the Modern World* (New York: Meridian Books, 1955), p. 20.

12. R. P. Blackmur, *Language as Gesture* (New York: Harcourt, Brace, 1952), p. 372. See also "A Burden for Critics," *The Lion and the Honeycomb* (New York: Harcourt, Brace, 1954), pp. 198–212.

13. John Crowe Ransom, "The Poetry of 1900–1950," *The Past Half Century in Literature* (National Council of the Teachers of English, 1952), pp. 12–18.

14. Cleanth Brooks, Foreword to *Critiques and Essays in Criticism,* ed. R. W. Stallman (New York: Ronald Press, 1949), p. xvi.

15. Howard Mumford Jones, "Literary Scholarship and Contemporary Criticism," *English Journal,* XXIII (1934), 755. An irony here is that Dr. Jones has since this time tended more and more to become a literary journalist.

16. Lionel Trilling, "The Farmer and the Cowboy Make Friends," *The Griffin,* V (1956), 12.

17. For an intelligent but unfriendly discussion of the *Short History* see Robert Marsh, "The 'Fallacy' of Universal Intention," *Modern Philology,* LV (May, 1958), 263–75.

18. Among the most important revaluative articles are Roy Harvey Pearce's "Historicism Once More," *Kenyon Review,* XX (Autumn, 1958), 554–91; Hyatt H. Waggoner's "The Current Revolt against the New Criticism," *Criticism,* I (Summer, 1959), 211–25; Walter Sutton's "The Contextualist Dilemma—or Fallacy?," *Journal of Aesthetics and Art Criticism,* XVII (December, 1958), 219–29; Mark Spilka's "The Necessary Stylist: A New Critical Revision," *Modern Fiction Studies,* VI (Winter, 1960–61), 281–97. For a similar theoretical critique tied to a piece of illustratively corrective practical criticism, see Robert M. Jordan's "The Limits of Allusion: Faulkner, Fielding, and Chaucer," *Criticism,* II (Summer, 1960), 278–305.

2. THE ROMANTICISM OF THE NEW CRITICISM

1. I. H. Hassan, "Criticism as Mimesis," *The South Atlantic Quarterly,* LV (1956), 475.

2. John Crowe Ransom, *The New Criticism* (Norfolk, Conn.: New Directions, 1941), p. 15. See also, for example, Cleanth Brooks on Romantic poetic theory and its resultant theories of "appreciation"

in his Foreword to *Critiques and Essays in Criticism* (New York: Ronald Press, 1949), p. xvi.

3. R. P. Blackmur, "Madame Bovary: Beauty Out of Place," *Kenyon Review*, XIII (1951), 478.

4. Hoyt Trowbridge in "Aristotle and the New Criticism," *The Sewanee Review*, LII (1944), 537-38, distinguishes historically two major methods of discourse—Aristotle's "inductive and analytical" method and Plato's "dialectical" method. He sees Plato's as "the method of almost all the standard critics, including the 'New Critics' of the past ten or fifteen years." He points out that the dialectical method is "speculative and *a priori*" and "applicable to any field of study."

5. R. P. Blackmur, "Dante's Ten Terms for the Treatment of the Treatise," *The Lion and the Honeycomb* (New York: Harcourt, Brace, 1954), p. 235.

6. I. A. Richards, *Coleridge on Imagination* (London, 1935; Bloomington: Indiana University Press, 1960), p. 230.

7. Allen Tate, "Narcissus as Narcissus," *The Man of Letters in the Modern World* (New York: Meridian Books, 1955), pp. 333-34.

8. Richards, *Coleridge on Imagination*, p. 230.

9. Philip Wheelwright, *The Burning Fountain* (Bloomington: Indiana University Press, 1954), p. 302.

10. Robert Penn Warren, "Knowledge and the Image of Man," *The Sewanee Review*, LXIII (1955), 192.

11. Eliseo Vivas, "What Is a Poem?," *Creation and Discovery* (New York: Noonday Press, 1954), p. 87.

12. Jacques Maritain, "Poetry's Dark Night," *Kenyon Review*, IX (1942), 158.

13. Blackmur, "Between the Numen and the Moha," *The Lion and the Honeycomb*, p. 297.

14. Robert B. Heilman, *This Great Stage: Image and Structure in King Lear* (Baton Rouge: Louisiana State University Press, 1948).

15. Robert Penn Warren, "A Poem of Pure Imagination," introduction to *The Rime of the Ancient Mariner* (New York: Reynal and Hitchcock, 1946).

16. I. A. Richards, *Science and Poetry* (New York: Norton, 1926), p. 95.

17. John Crowe Ransom, "Forms and Citizens," *The World's Body* (New York: Scribner, 1938), p. 43.

18. John Crowe Ransom, "Poetry: A Note on Ontology," *The World's Body*, p. 140.

19. *The Critical Performance*, ed. Stanley Edgar Hyman (New York: Vintage Books, 1956), pp. 191–204. See especially the passage elaborated from Blackmur, pp. 198–99.

20. Ransom, *The New Criticism*, p. 204.

21. John Crowe Ransom, "Humanism at Chicago," *Poems and Essays* (New York: Vintage Books, 1955), p. 91.

22. Ransom, *The New Criticism*, p. 205.

23. R. P. Blackmur, "The Enabling Act of Criticism," in *Critiques and Essays in Criticism*, ed. R. W. Stallman (New York: Ronald Press, 1949), pp. 412–15. In "Humanism and Symbolic Imagination, Notes on Re-reading Irving Babbitt," *The Lion and the Honeycomb*, pp. 145–61, Blackmur discusses Babbitt's inadequacies of imagination. Babbitt is the foil for Blackmur's urgent insistence that as moderns we need "a secular equivalent of the religious imagination" (p. 152).

24. R. P. Blackmur, "A Burden for Critics," *The Lion and the Honeycomb*, pp. 201–202. R. W. B. Lewis, in "Casella as Critic: A Note on R. P. Blackmur," *Kenyon Review*, XIII (1951), 458–74, takes account of Blackmur's relation to Arnold, particularly in "A Burden for Critics." But he is mostly concerned to see that no one reads Blackmur as following Arnold "in any simplified way" (p. 471). There could be no doubt that Blackmur is more completely under the influence of the Muses than was Arnold, and that Arnold probably wouldn't have understood a word Blackmur said.

25. Murray Krieger has noted in *The New Apologists for Poetry* (Minneapolis: University of Minnesota Press, 1956), p. 140, that the stress on complexity can tend toward a "reckless romanticism," and that its origin in "the science-poetry dichotomy" is of course a romantic one.

3. I. A. RICHARDS: FROM LABORATORY TO IMAGINATION

1. John Crowe Ransom, "A Psychologist Looks at Poetry," *The World's Body* (New York: Scribner, 1938), p. 155.

2. I. A. Richards, *Principles of Literary Criticism* (New York: Harcourt, Brace, 1949), p. 3.

3. *Ibid.*, pp. 40, 20.

4. *Ibid.*, p. 23.

5. I. A. Richards, *Science and Poetry* (New York: Norton, 1926), p. 74.

6. I. A. Richards, *Practical Criticism* (New York: Harvest Books, 1956), p. 284.

7. In the chapter on "Art, Play and Civilization" (*Principles of Literary Criticism*, pp. 223–38) Richards had already begun to envision, from the vantage point of this theory, the enormous role to be played by the arts in a projected possible educational revolution.

8. *Ibid.*, p. 229.

9. Ransom, "A Psychologist Looks at Poetry," p. 155.

10. Richards, *Principles of Literary Criticism*, pp. 254–60.

11. *Ibid.*, pp. 283–84.

12. I. A. Richards, "Between Truth and Truth," *Symposium*, II (1931), 228–29.

13. Cleanth Brooks, "The Problem of Belief and the Problem of Cognition," *The Well Wrought Urn* (New York: Harvest Books, 1955), p. 259.

14. Ransom, "A Psychologist Looks at Poetry," pp. 163–64; and *The New Criticism* (Norfolk, Conn.: New Directions, 1941), pp. 74–75.

15. Walter Ong, "The Meaning of the New Criticism," in *Twentieth Century English*, ed. W. S. Knickerbocker (New York: Philosophical Library, 1946), p. 358.

16. I. A. Richards, *Coleridge on Imagination* (London, 1935; Bloomington: Indiana University Press, 1960), p. 69.

17. I. A. Richards, "Responsibilities in the Teaching of English," *Speculative Instruments* (Chicago: University of Chicago Press, 1955), p. 105.

18. I. A. Richards, *The Philosophy of Rhetoric* (New York: Oxford University Press, 1936), p. 131.

19. *Ibid.*, p. 13.

20. Richards, *Coleridge on Imagination*, p. 47.

21. Richards, "Emotive Meaning Again," *Speculative Instruments*, pp. 55–56.

22. Richards, *Coleridge on Imagination*, p. 171. Richards' using the word "soul," while it is a manner of speaking picked up from Coleridge, is a telling symptom of change. The word would not have been very comfortable in Richards' earlier contexts.

23. *Ibid.*, pp. 227–29. This may be the explanation for Stanley

Hyman's claim in *The Armed Vision* (New York: Knopf, 1948), pp. 312, 343, that with *The Philosophy of Rhetoric* Richards' interest dropped from poetry to Basic English and education. This is only technically true, of course. For the schoolmaster is still Coleridge as philosopher, poet, psychologist, perhaps even scientist—with special assistance from certain Oriental thinkers, and Plato and his dialectical method.

24. F. R. Leavis, review of *Coleridge on Imagination, Scrutiny,* III (1935), 390.

25. Richards, *Speculative Instruments,* p. 48.

26. *Ibid.,* p. 44, n. 1.

27. *Ibid.,* p. 53, n. 1.

28. Allen Tate, "Literature as Knowledge," *The Man of Letters in the Modern World* (New York: Meridian Books, 1955), p. 63.

4. ELISEO VIVAS: FROM NATURE TO SPIRIT

1. Eliseo Vivas, "The Aesthetic Judgment," *The Journal of Philosophy,* XXXIII (1936), 68.

2. John Crowe Ransom, "Criticism as Pure Speculation," in *The Intent of the Critic,* ed. Donald A. Stauffer (Princeton: Princeton University Press, 1941), 96.

3. Eliseo Vivas, "Lawrence's Problems," *Kenyon Review,* III (1941), 94.

4. Eliseo Vivas, "Reply to Mr. Wheelwright," *Kenyon Review,* IV (1942), 97.

5. *Ibid.,* p. 93.

6. Henry D. Aiken, "Aesthetics on the Stretch," *Kenyon Review,* XVIII (1955), 633.

7. Eliseo Vivas, *The Moral Life and the Ethical Life* (Chicago: University of Chicago Press, 1950), p. ix.

8. *Ibid.,* note, p. 366.

9. Eliseo Vivas, "On Symbolism," *Kenyon Review,* V (1943), 301–304.

10. Eliseo Vivas, "Two Notes on the New Naturalism," *The Sewanee Review,* LVI (1948), 477–509.

11. Vivas, *The Moral Life and the Ethical Life,* p. vii.

12. Eliseo Vivas, "Kafka's Distorted Mask," *Creation and Discovery* (New York: Noonday Press, 1955), pp. 29–46. Six of the seventeen

essays in this volume were published before 1948. But in the preface Vivas admits to having revised the earlier essays "in order to bring them closer to what I take to be a maturer grasp of the truth than I once had" (p. xiii). It is significant that he does not reprint the obviously unrevisable essay on Lawrence; but see his recent book on Lawrence (n. 41, below).

13. Vivas, "The Dimensions of Reality in *The Brothers Karamazov*," *ibid.*, p. 56.

14. Vivas, "Allen Tate as Man of Letters," *ibid.*, p. 277.

15. Vivas, "Two Notes on the New Naturalism," *ibid.*, p. 507.

16. Eliseo Vivas, "The Nature of Aesthetics," in *The Return to Reason*, ed. John Wild (Chicago: University of Chicago Press, 1953), p. 217.

17. Vivas, "Two Notes on the New Naturalism," p. 493.

18. Vivas, *Creation and Discovery*, n. 3, p. 290.

19. *Ibid.*, pp. 84–85.

20. *Ibid.*, p. xii.

21. Vivas, "The Objective Correlative of T. S. Eliot," *Creation and Discovery*, p. 188. The proximity—no doubt entirely unwitting—of some of Vivas' sentiments to those of Shelley is strikingly borne out in his examination of the aesthetics of Elijah Jordan ("Jordan's Defense of Poetry," *Creation and Discovery*, pp. 229–247). If we may judge from Vivas' numerous quotations, Jordan outdoes Shelley in the gigantism of his claims for poetry. And Vivas lauds Jordan's work as a "tremendous achievement" (p. 247).

22. Sidney Hook, "A Case Study in Anti-Secularism," *Partisan Review*, XVIII (March–April, 1951), 232–45. Needless to say Hook's examination contains other than purely logical criteria of criticism. He, like Vivas, has a special "viewpoint," essentially that of the New Naturalism.

23. Aiken, "Aesthetics on the Stretch," p. 633.

24. Vivas, *The Moral Life and the Ethical Life*, p. 217.

25. Eliseo Vivas, "A Note on Value," *The Journal of Philosophy*, XXXIII (1936), 568.

26. Vivas, "The Aesthetic Judgment," p. 66.

27. Vivas, *The Moral Life and the Ethical Life*, p. 76.

28. *Ibid.*, p. 330. My italics. It may be a little surprising to learn a few pages later that Vivas' rational consciousness, after displaying this agility, feels that it cannot know "with the same kind of positive

knowledge that we know of its sojourn in the body, what its fate is when it abandons its fleshly abode" (p. 334).

29. *Ibid.*, p. 331.

30. Vivas, "Reply to Mr. Wheelwright," p. 96.

31. Vivas, "What is a Poem?," *Creation and Discovery*, p. 91.

32. Vivas, "Four Notes on I. A. Richards' Aesthetic Theory," *Creation and Discovery*, p. 218. Since Vivas admits to having revised his separately published essays for their publication together in *Creation and Discovery*, it seems fair enough to hold him accountable here.

33. Vivas, "What is a Poem?," pp. 73–75.

34. Vivas, *Creation and Discovery*, p. 137.

35. *Ibid.*, p. 89.

36. Vivas, *The Moral Life and the Ethical Life*, p. 221.

37. Eliseo Vivas, "A Semantics for Humanists," *The Sewanee Review*, LXIII (1955), 317.

38. The long review of *The Moral Life and the Ethical Life* by Sidney Hook (see above, n. 22), takes up in detail the full range of implications—from the political to the theological—of Vivas' case of reaction.

39. Vivas, *The Moral Life and the Ethical Life*, pp. 339, 341.

40. *Ibid.*, p. 250.

41. Eliseo Vivas, *D. H. Lawrence: The Triumph and Failure of Art* (Evanston, Ill.: Northwestern University Press, 1960), pp. xiv, x, and 81–85.

42. Vivas, *The Moral Life and the Ethical Life*, p. 346.

43. A recent bit of spiritual autobiography by Vivas is his tribute to Allen Tate in the special issue of *Sewanee Review* published in honor of Tate's sixtieth birthday (LXVII [1959], 560–66). This piece seems generally to confirm the interpretation of Vivas' spiritual and intellectual history given here.

5. R. P. BLACKMUR: FROM CRITICISM TO MYSTICISM

1. R. P. Blackmur, "Judgment, Form, Sensibility," *Kenyon Review*, X (1948), 314.

2. R. P. Blackmur, ed., *The Art of the Novel* (New York and London: Scribner, 1934), p. xiii.

3. *Ibid.*, p. xi.

4. Howard Mumford Jones, "The Limits of Contemporary Criticism," *The Saturday Review of Literature*, XXIV (September 6, 1941), 3.

5. Stanley Edgar Hyman, *The Armed Vision* (New York: Knopf, 1948), p. 269.

6. Alfred Kazin, *On Native Grounds* (New York: Reynal and Hitchcock, 1942), p. 439.

7. John Crowe Ransom, "Ubiquitous Moralists," *Kenyon Review*, III (1941), 96–97.

8. R. P. Blackmur, "A Critic's Job of Work," *Language as Gesture* (New York: Harcourt, Brace, 1952), p. 396.

9. Stanley Edgar Hyman in *The Armed Vision* praises Blackmur's comprehensiveness and diligence as "not so much a unique method as a unique habit of mind, a capacity for painstaking investigation" (p. 239). But it is significant that Hyman is referring in this context to essays published before 1940, and especially to those in Blackmur's first collection, *The Double Agent*, published in 1935. (See *The Armed Vision*, p. 244.)

10. Malcolm Cowley, *The Literary Situation* (New York: Viking, 1954), p. 11.

11. Hugh Holman, "The Defense of Art: Criticism Since 1930," in *The Development of American Literary Criticism*, ed. Floyd Stovall (Chapel Hill: University of North Carolina Press, 1955), p. 237.

12. John Crowe Ransom, "More Than Gesture," *Poems and Essays* (New York: Vintage Books, 1955), pp. 102–108.

13. Murray Krieger, *The New Apologists for Poetry* (Minneapolis: University of Minnesota Press, 1956), p. 9.

14. Harry Levin in *The New Republic*, CIII (December 23, 1940), 906.

15. Irving Howe, "Magazine Chronicle," *Partisan Review*, XVI (January–June, 1949), 423.

16. It must be borne in mind, of course, that because Blackmur has always used "reason"-words very loosely and inconsistently, we can generalize about his use of them only relatively and approximately.

17. R. P. Blackmur, "The Imagination Crowned," *The Nation*, CXL (April 10, 1935), 423.

18. Blackmur, *Language as Gesture*, pp. 286–300.

19. R. P. Blackmur, "Notes on E. E. Cummings' Language," *The Double Agent* (New York: Arrow Editions, 1935), pp. 1–2, 28.

20. Blackmur, "Emily Dickinson, Notes on Prejudice and Fact," *Language as Gesture*, p. 30.

21. Blackmur, "Notes on E. E. Cummings' Language," pp. 20–21.

22. Hyman, *The Armed Vision*, p. 267.

23. R. P. Blackmur, "Humanism and Symbolic Imagination," *The Lion and the Honeycomb* (New York: Harcourt, Brace, 1954), p. 161.

24. Blackmur, "W. B. Yeats: Between Myth and Philosophy," *Language as Gesture*, p. 112.

25. Blackmur, "The Artist as Hero: A Disconsolate Chimera," *The Lion and the Honeycomb*, p. 47.

26. Blackmur, *The Lion and the Honeycomb*, p. 153.

27. *Ibid.*, p. 212.

28. *Ibid.*, pp. 294, 302–303.

29. R. P. Blackmur, "The Language of Silence," *The Sewanee Review*, LXIII (1955), 401.

30. *Ibid.*, p. 386.

31. *Ibid.*, p. 391.

32. *Ibid.*, p. 386.

33. Hyman, *The Armed Vision*, pp. 261–62.

34. R. P. Blackmur, "The Jew in Search of a Son," *The Virginia Quarterly Review*, XXIV (1948), 96–116.

35. Blackmur, "A Burden for Critics," *The Lion and the Honeycomb*, p. 206.

36. Blackmur, *The Lion and the Honeycomb*, pp. 191, 195.

37. John Crowe Ransom, "The Understanding of Fiction," *Kenyon Review*, XII (1950), 214.

38. R. P. Blackmur, "It Is Later Than He Thinks," *The Expense of Greatness* (New York: Arrow Editions, 1940), p. 241.

39. Blackmur, *The Lion and the Honeycomb*, p. 184.

40. *Ibid.*, p. 293.

41. Blackmur, *Language as Gesture*, p. 398–99.

42. Blackmur, "Unappeasable and Peregrine, Behavior in the 'Four Quartets,'" *Language as Gesture*, p. 205.

43. R. P. Blackmur, "The Sacred Fount," *Kenyon Review*, IV (1942), 344.

44. Blackmur, "A Burden for Critics," *The Lion and the Honeycomb*, pp. 210–11.

45. *Ibid.*, p. 305.

46. R. P. Blackmur, "*Anna Karenina;* The Dialectics of Incarnation," *Kenyon Review,* XVII (1955), 433.

47. *Ibid.,* p. 440. Sometimes the transference of functions flows in the opposite direction—from poetry or art, back out to the institutions, which regain their functions in the degree that they are poetry. In "Reflections of Toynbee," *Kenyon Review,* XVII (1955), 357-70, Toynbee's quality as a philosopher of history is due not to his mastery of the philosopher's or the historian's skills but to his imaginative grasp of history. He is to Blackmur the "historian-as-poet" (p. 365).

48. Hyman, *The Armed Vision,* p. 266.

49. R. W. B. Lewis, "Casella as Critic: A Note on R. P. Blackmur," *Kenyon Review,* XIII (1951), 473-74.

50. *Ibid.,* p. 474.

51. Blackmur, "Humanism and Symbolic Imagination," *The Lion and the Honeycomb,* p. 147.

52. Howe, "Magazine Chronicle," p. 423.

6. ALLEN TATE: FROM THE OLD SOUTH TO
CATHOLIC ORTHODOXY

1. Allen Tate, "The Man of Letters in the Modern World," *The Man of Letters in the Modern World* (New York: Meridian Books, 1955), p. 12.

2. Allen Tate, *Reactionary Essays* (New York: Scribner, 1936), pp. 83-112.

3. Tate, "The Symbolic Imagination," *The Man of Letters in the Modern World,* p. 96.

4. *Ibid.,* p. 97.

5. Tate, "The Angelic Imagination," *The Man of Letters in the Modern World,* pp. 129, 131.

6. Tate, "Narcissus as Narcissus," *The Man of Letters in the Modern World,* p. 337.

7. Tate, "The Angelic Imagination," p. 131.

8. Allen Tate, "Confusion and Poetry," *The Sewanee Review,* XXXVIII (April, 1930), 134-35.

9. Kathleen Nott, *The Emperor's Clothes* (Bloomington: Indiana University Press, 1954), p. 166.

10. Alfred Kazin, *On Native Grounds* (New York: Reynal and Hitchcock, 1942), pp. 442-43.

11. R. P. Blackmur, "Notes on Eleven Poets," *Kenyon Review*, VII (1945), 343–45.

12. Allen Tate, "What Is a Traditional Society?," *Reason in Madness* (New York: Putnam, 1941), pp. 217–30.

13. Tate, "The New Provincialism," *The Man of Letters in the Modern World*, p. 330. An interesting example of Tate's devotion to some of these classic values appeared in the pages of *Partisan Review* when during the Pound-Bollingen Award controversy Tate interpreted William Barrett's criticism of the committee's decision as a charge against him of anti-Semitism. "I hope," he wrote in answer, "that persons who wish to accuse me of cowardice and dishonor will do so henceforth personally, in my presence, so that I may dispose of the charge at some other level than that of public discussion. Courage and honor are not subjects of literary controversy, but occasions of action." But Barrett wanted to get on with the moral discussion, and dismissed Tate's apparent challenge to a personal duel as "strictly extracurricular." (*Partisan Review*, XVI [1949], pp. 520–21.)

14. Tate, *The Man of Letters in the Modern World*, p. 309.

15. Allen Tate, "Religion and the Old South," *On the Limits of Poetry* (New York: Alan Swallow, 1948), p. 322.

16. Kazin, *On Native Grounds*, p. 428.

17. Tate, "Our Cousin, Mr. Poe," *The Man of Letters in the Modern World*, p. 135.

18. Tate, *The Man of Letters in the Modern World*, p. 331.

19. Vivienne Koch, "The Poetry of Allen Tate," *The Kenyon Critics*, ed. John Crowe Ransom (Cleveland: World, 1951), pp. 169–81.

20. John Paul Pritchard, *Criticism in America* (Norman: University of Oklahoma Press, 1956), pp. 249–50; and Frederick B. Rainsberry, "The Irony of Objectivity in the New Criticism," unpublished dissertation (Michigan State University, 1953), p. 106.

21. Tate, "Confusion and Poetry," p. 142.

22. See, for example, the closing paragraph of "To Whom Is the Poet Responsible?," *The Man of Letters in the Modern World*, p. 33.

23. Kazin, *On Native Grounds*, p. 442.

24. F. X. Roellinger, "Two Theories of Poetry as Knowledge," *The Southern Review*, VII (1942), 694.

25. Monroe K. Spears, "The Criticism of Allen Tate," *The Sewanee Review*, LVII (1949), 327.

26. Allen Tate, "Poetry and the Absolute," *The Sewanee Review,* XXXV (1927), 41–52.

27. Tate, *The Man of Letters in the Modern World,* p. 20.

28. Tate, "Is Literary Criticism Possible?," *The Man of Letters in the Modern World,* p. 174.

29. Allen Tate, "The Critic's Business," *The Forlorn Demon* (Chicago: Regnery, 1953), p. 162.

30. Tate, *The Man of Letters in the Modern World,* p. 20.

31. Tate, "Confusion and Poetry," p. 141.

32. Tate, *The Man of Letters in the Modern World,* pp. 144–45.

33. Tate, "Confusion and Poetry," p. 137.

34. *Ibid.,* p. 136.

35. Tate, "Liberalism and Tradition," *Reason in Madness,* p. 206.

36. Allen Tate, "To Ford Madox Ford," *Chimera,* I (1943), 19–20; and "Hart Crane," and "Crane: The Poet as Hero," *The Man of Letters in the Modern World,* pp. 283–94, 295–98.

37. Tate, *Reason in Madness,* p. 202.

38. Allen Tate, "The New Criticism," *The American Scholar,* XX (1950–51), 93; and *Partisan Review,* XVII (1950), 250–53.

39. Allen Tate, "Orthodoxy and the Standard of Literature," *The New Republic,* CXXVIII (January 5, 1953), 24–25.

40. Katherine Bregy, "Allen Tate: Paradoxical Pilgrim," *Catholic World,* CLXXX (1953), 121–22.

41. Allen Tate, "Christ and the Unicorn," *The Sewanee Review,* LXIII (1955), p. 178.

7. POETRY AS KNOWLEDGE

1. Murray Krieger, *The New Apologists for Poetry* (Minneapolis: University of Minnesota Press, 1956), p. 35.

2. Stanley Edgar Hyman, *The Armed Vision* (New York: Knopf, 1948), p. 11.

3. F. R. Leavis, "Coleridge in Criticism," *Scrutiny,* IX (1940), 69.

4. R. S. Crane, Prefatory Note to "Two Essays in Practical Criticism," *The University Review,* VIII (1942), 199.

5. Though he notes Blackmur's admiration for Kenneth Burke, another Coleridge-influenced critic, Hyman judges that "alone of serious contemporary critics, Blackmur seems to have been little

affected by Coleridge and the Biographia" (The Armed Vision, p. 253).

6. The philosophical source studies have tended so far to take the form of unpublished dissertations; see especially William J. Handy, "Poetry as Knowledge: The Kantian Tradition in Modern Literary Theory" (University of Oklahoma, 1954), and Frederick B. Rainsberry, "The Irony of Objectivity in the New Criticism" (Michigan State University, 1953). See also Sholom J. Kahn, "What Does a Critic Analyze?," Philosophy and Phenomenological Research, XIII (1952), 237–45.

7. John Crowe Ransom, "A Psychologist Looks at Poetry," The World's Body (New York: Scribner, 1938), p. 157.

8. John Crowe Ransom, "Humanism at Chicago," Poems and Essays (New York: Vintage Books, 1955), p. 92.

9. Ransom, "The Concrete Universal: Observations of the Understanding of Poetry," Poems and Essays, p. 159.

10. Ibid., p. 161.

11. R. P. Blackmur, "The Loose and Baggy Monsters of Henry James," The Lion and the Honeycomb (New York: Harcourt, Brace, 1954), p. 269.

12. Ransom, "Why Critics Don't Go Mad," Poems and Essays, p. 150. Richards claimed, I think rightly, in Principles of Literary Criticism (New York: Harcourt, Brace, 1950), n. 4, pp. 255–56, that Croce's appeal has been largely to amateurs in aesthetics, to "the man of letters and the dilettante," and that he "has been ignored by serious students of the mind."

13. Blackmur mentions both incidentally as having viewpoints agreeable to his own in "A Burden for Critics" (The Lion and the Honeycomb, p. 208).

14. Eliseo Vivas, The Moral Life and the Ethical Life (Chicago: University of Chicago Press, 1950), pp. x–xi.

15. Eliseo Vivas, "The Neo-Aristotelians of Chicago," The Sewanee Review, LXI (1953), 142.

16. Eliseo Vivas, "What is a Poem?" Creation and Discovery (New York: Noonday Press, 1954), p. 80.

17. Ransom, "The Mimetic Principle," The World's Body, p. 200.

18. In 1954 Ransom said of his term "texture" that he had "no sooner uttered it than it struck me as a flat and inadequate figure for that vivid and easily felt part of a poem which we associate peculiarly

with poetic language." ("The Concrete Universal: Observations on the Understanding of Poetry," *Kenyon Review*, XVI [1954], 559.)

19. John Crowe Ransom, *The New Criticism* (Norfolk: Conn.: New Directions, 1941), pp. 74–75.

20. Ransom, "A Psychologist Looks at Poetry," *The World's Body*, p. 156.

21. In *The New Criticism* Ransom flatly stated that texture "is the thing that peculiarly qualifies a discourse as being poetic; it is its differentia" (p. 220).

22. Ransom, "Art Worries the Naturalists," *Kenyon Review*, VII (1945), 293.

23. Ransom, "Poetry: The Formal Analysis," *Kenyon Review*, IX (1947), 447.

24. F. X. Roellinger, "Two Theories of Poetry as Knowledge," *Southern Review*, VII (1942), 701.

25. Ransom, *The New Criticism*, p. 281.

26. Roellinger, "Two Theories of Poetry as Knowledge," p. 697. Richard Fogle, in "Romantic Bards and Metaphysical Reviewers," *ELH*, XII (1945), 223, made the same objection to T. E. Hulme's very similar poetics. We may discern the unavailability of convincing defenses against such objections in Ransom's answer to the idea that a photograph may be fuller and more faithful to its object than a painting, if it is the *object* in all its textural richness and variety that is important. The photograph, Ransom weakly responded, is got by "actions so characterless that they indicate no attitude necessarily, no love; but the painting reveals the arduous pains of the artist" ("The Mimetic Principle," *The World's Body*, p. 209). Which is quite another matter indeed.

27. Ransom, "A Psychologist Looks at Poetry," p. 158.

28. John Crowe Ransom, "The Pragmatics of Art," *Kenyon Review*, II (1940), 84.

29. John Crowe Ransom, "Criticism as Pure Speculation," in *The Intent of the Critic*, ed. Donald A. Stauffer (Princeton: Princeton University Press, 1941), pp. 91–124.

30. See, for example, John Crowe Ransom, "The Literary Criticism of Aristotle," in *Lectures in Criticism*, ed. Huntington Cairns (New York: 1949), pp. 15–42; and "The Concrete Universal: Observations on the Understanding of Poetry," *Kenyon Review*, XVI (1954), 554–64, and *Poems and Essays*, pp. 159–85.

31. More recently Ransom has been describing the poem as having a "trinitarian" existence, bringing together three worlds—those of things, of rational abstraction, and of the "ideal"—rather than two worlds. But this refinement of the vehicle of Ransom's theory does not appear to change its tenor essentially. The theory still centers on the nature of the relation between particulars and universals, even though the universals are seen now to be of two orders.

32. Yvor Winters, "John Crowe Ransom, or Thunder Without God," *In Defense of Reason* (Denver: 1947), pp. 513–18.

33. Herbert Muller, "The New Criticism in Poetry," *Southern Review*, VI (1941), 813.

34. Darrell Abell, "Intellectual Criticism," *The American Scholar*, XII (1943), 425.

35. René Wellek and Austin Warren, *Theory of Literature* (New York: Harcourt, Brace, 1949), pp. 151–58, and Cleanth Brooks, "The Heresy of Paraphrase," *The Well Wrought Urn* (New York: Harvest Books, 1955), p. 203.

36. Blackmur, "The Loose and Baggy Monsters of Henry James," pp. 268–69.

37. Leslie Fiedler, "In the Beginning was the Word: Mythos or Logos?," *The Sewanee Review*, LXIII (1955), 409–10.

38. Robert Penn Warren, "Knowledge and the Image of Man," *The Sewanee Review*, LXIII (1955), 190–91.

39. Allen Tate, "The Man of Letters in the Modern World," *The Man of Letters in the Modern World* (New York: Meridian Books, 1955), p. 18. Compare Tate's earlier "Literature as Knowledge," *ibid.*, p. 62, where poetry is "complete" knowledge, but knowledge which is neither of "the world of verifiable science nor a projection of ourselves." I am not able to classify this idea with much conviction because I am not certain what he wants to mean; but it sounds more like an ontological knowledge than anything else. W. K. Wimsatt, Jr., has objected to the "incarnation" theory of poetry suggested in the work of the converted Tate and certain other Catholic writers on the ground that it is at best a mere metaphor: "It is a little less than making a structure of words a substance or even a good analogy to, or a dependent upon, a historical or personal incarnation." ("Criticism Today: A Report From America," *Essays in Criticism*, VI [1956], 16).

40. I. A. Richards, "The Future of the Humanities in General Education," *Speculative Instruments* (Chicago: University of Chicago Press, 1955), p. 59.

41. Suzanne K. Langer, *Feeling and Form* (New York: Scribner, 1953), p. 374.

42. Vivas, *Creation and Discovery*, pp. 125–26.

43. Vivas, "The Objective Correlative of T. S. Eliot," *ibid.*, p. 187.

44. Vivas, "What Is a Poem?", *ibid.*, p. 80.

45. Philip Wheelwright, *The Burning Fountain* (Bloomington: Indiana University Press, 1954), p. 302.

46. Yvor Winters, "John Crowe Ransom," *In Defense of Reason*, p. 523.

47. Murray Krieger, *The New Apologists for Poetry*, p. 189. See also Ernest Nagle on Mrs. Langer in *The Journal of Philosophy*, XL (1953), 329.

48. C. K. Ogden and I. A. Richards, *The Meaning of Meaning* (New York: Harcourt, Brace, 1943), p. 151.

49. *Ibid.*, p. 157.

50. Krieger, *The New Apologists for Poetry*, p. 190.

8. CRITICISM AS POETRY

1. Louis Grudin, *Mr. Eliot among the Nightingales* (Paris: L. Drake, 1932), p. 3.

2. I. A. Richards, *Principles of Literary Criticism* (New York: Harcourt, Brace, 1950), p. 40.

3. John Crowe Ransom, "Humanism at Chicago," *Poems and Essays* (New York: Vintage Books, 1955), p. 89.

4. R. P. Blackmur, "Between the Numen and the Moha," *The Lion and the Honeycomb* (New York: Harcourt, Brace, 1954), p. 289.

5. *Ibid.*, p. 292.

6. Blackmur, "The Loose and Baggy Monsters of Henry James," *The Lion and the Honeycomb*, p. 279.

7. Blackmur, "Between the Numen and the Moha," p. 294.

8. R. P. Blackmur, "The Great Grasp of Unreason," *Hudson Review*, IX (1956–57), 498.

9. Blackmur, "Notes on Four Categories in Criticism," *The Lion and the Honeycomb*, p. 224.

10. R. P. Blackmur, "The Language of Silence," *The Sewanee Review*, LXIII (1955), 391.

11. R. P. Blackmur, "Language as Gesture," *Language as Gesture* (New York: Harcourt, Brace, 1952), pp. 3–24.

12. Grudin, *Mr. Eliot Among the Nightingales*, p. 9.

13. Blackmur, "A Burden for Critics," *The Lion and the Honeycomb*, p. 211.

14. Blackmur, "Language as Gesture," p. 6.

15. R. P. Blackmur, "Madame Bovary: Beauty Out of Place," *Kenyon Review*, XIII (1951), 476.

16. Blackmur, "The Loose and Baggy Monsters of Henry James," p. 284.

17. Blackmur, "Dante's Ten Terms for the Treatment of the Treatise," *The Lion and the Honeycomb*, p. 228.

18. Kathleen Nott, *The Emperor's Clothes* (Bloomington: Indiana University Press, 1954), p. 58.

19. John Crowe Ransom, *God without Thunder* (New York: Harcourt, Brace, 1930), p. 32.

20. *Ibid.*, p. 59. Ransom sometimes flounders between the poles of his dialectic in *God without Thunder* and sounds the wrong cry. On page 255, in contradiction, it seems, to all that he has been claiming, he declares that "scientific knowledge is that type of knowledge which occupies itself with exact comparisons and precise measurements."

21. *Ibid.*, p. 114.

22. Leslie Fiedler, "In the Beginning Was the Word: Mythos or Logos?," *The Sewanee Review*, LXIII (1955), 412.

23. Eliseo Vivas, *The Moral Life and the Ethical Life* (Chicago: University of Chicago Press, 1950), p. 19.

24. *Ibid.*, p. 315.

25. Ransom, *God without Thunder*, p. 34.

26. Cleanth Brooks, *Modern Poetry and the Tradition* (Chapel Hill: University of North Carolina Press, 1939), p. 174. Kathleen Nott has an interesting comment on the logic of such restrictions. "When there are any phenomena at all," she observes, "there is the possibility of scientific inquiry, with or without test-tubes and calipers. Indeed, because unity of investigation, the practice of asking

questions in such a way that the possibility of an answer is implicit, is an essential of science, all phenomena whatsoever must at least theoretically demand scientific inquiry" (*The Emperor's Clothes*, p. 61). Brooks' sort of rhetoric is a little dangerous, then, since he and other "Two Truths" people might be understood as implying that religion, considered epistemologically, is without phenomena.

27. Blackmur, *The Lion and the Honeycomb*, p. 220.

28. *Ibid.*, p. 223.

29. Blackmur, "Unappeasable and Peregrine; Behavior and the 'Four Quartets'," *Language as Gesture*, p. 205.

30. Blackmur, "The Loose and Baggy Monsters of Henry James," p. 280.

31. *Ibid.*, p. 281.

32. Charles Morris, "Comments on Mysticism and Its Language," *ETC.: A Review of General Semantics*, IX (1951), 6–8.

33. Suzanne K. Langer, *Feeling and Form* (New York: Scribner, 1953), p. 32.

34. Karl Shapiro, "A Farewell to Criticism," *Poetry, A Magazine of Verse*, LXXI (1948), 210. (Italics mine.)

35. Allen Tate, "Narcissus as Narcissus," *The Man of Letters in the Modern World* (New York: Meridian Books, 1955), pp. 333–34 (Italics mine.)

36. Cleanth Brooks. *The Well Wrought Urn* (New York: Harvest Books, 1947), p. 203. (Italics mine.)

37. *Ibid.*, p. 195. (Italics mine.)

38. *Ibid.*, p. 203.

39. John Crowe Ransom, "Poetry: A Note on Ontology," *The World's Body* (New York: Scribners, 1938), p. 130.

40. Ransom, *God without Thunder*, p. 219.

41. Ransom, "Why Critics Don't Go Mad," *Poems and Essays*, p. 155.

42. Blackmur, "Lord Tennyson's Scissors: 1912–1950," *Language as Gesture*, pp. 422–23.

43. Tate, "Hart Crane," *The Man of Letters in the Modern World*, pp. 283–94.

44. Tate, "Techniques of Fiction," *ibid.*, pp. 84–85.

45. Ransom, *The World's Body*, p. vii.

46. Blackmur, "A Critic's Job of Work," *Language as Gesture*, p. 372.

47. Tate, *The Man of Letters in the Modern World*, p. 6.

48. Ransom, "Humanism at Chicago," p. 89.

49. Tate, "Techniques of Fiction," p. 81. This is also, of course, clever incidental *criticism* of Thackeray.

50. Blackmur, "The Expense of Greatness," *The Lion and the Honeycomb*, p. 95.

51. Alfred Kazin, *On Native Grounds* (New York, 1942), p. 426.

52. Blackmur, "Between the Numen and the Moha," p. 291.

53. Tate, *The Man of Letters in the Modern World*, p. 174.

54. Blackmur, "A Critic's Job of Work," p. 378. Hyman observes in *The Armed Vision* (New York: Knopf, 1948), p. 293, that Empson, drawing from the skeptical rationalism of the early Richards, is a definite exception to those who hold that the poem is an inexhaustible and ultimately unanalyzable object.

55. Eliseo Vivas, *Creation and Disovery* (New York: Noonday Press, 1954), p. 88.

56. Blackmur, "The Method of Marianne Moore," *Language as Gesture*, p. 260.

57. Blackmur, "The Later Poetry of W. B. Yeats," *ibid.*, p. 80.

58. Tate, "The Hovering Fly," *The Man of Letters in the Modern World*, p. 147.

59. Blackmur, "W. B. Yeats: Between Myth and Philosophy," *Language as Gesture*, pp. 110–12.

60. Vivas, "Literature as Knowledge," *Creation and Discovery*, p. 104.

61. Blackmur, "Humanism and Symbolic Imagination," *The Lion and the Honeycomb*, p. 152.

62. I. A. Richards, "Poetry as an Instrument of Research," *Speculative Instruments* (Chicago: University of Chicago Press, 1955), p. 150.

63. Robert Penn Warren, "Pure and Impure Poetry," in *Critiques and Essays in Criticism*, ed. Robert W. Stallman (New York: Ronald Press, 1949), p. 86.

64. *Ibid.*, p. 85.

65. Fiedler, "In the Beginning Was the Word," p. 409.

66. Tate, *The Man of Letters in the Modern World*, p. 18.

67. In *Mr. Eliot Among the Nightingales*, p. 22, Louis Grudin remarks that this "emotional beatitude, reaching its climax in the capitalized words, is due to the sense of dealing in mysteries, in a divinely ordered, impenetrable affair."

68. Blackmur, "Toward a Modus Vivendi," *The Lion and the Honeycomb*, pp. 3–31.

69. Tate, "The Symbolic Imagination," *The Man of Letters in the Modern World*, p. 99.

70. Robert Gorham Davis, "The New Criticism and the Democratic Tradition," *The American Scholar*, XIX (1949–50), 17.

71. Kazin, *On Native Grounds*, p. 402.

72. Wallace W. Douglas, "The Solemn Style of Modern Critics," *The American Scholar*, XXIII (1953–54), 52.

73. John Crowe Ransom, "The Strange Music of English Verse," *Kenyon Review*, XVIII (1956), 476. See also "Humanism at Chicago" and "Why Critics Don't Go Mad," *Poems and Essays*, pp. 99–101 and 157 respectively.

74. Blackmur, "Between the Numen and the Moha," pp. 297–98.

75. Blackmur, *The Lion and the Honeycomb*, p. 207.

76. *Ibid.*, p. 212.

77. Morgan Blum, "The Fugitive Particular: John Crowe Ransom, Critic," *Western Review*, XIV (1950), 86.

78. Grudin, *Mr. Eliot Among the Nightingales*, p. 32.

79. Douglas, "The Solemn Style," p. 55.

80. Cleanth Brooks, Foreword to *Critiques and Essays in Criticism*, ed. R. W. Stallman (New York: Ronald Press, 1949), p. xviii.

81. Allen Tate, Preface to *On the Limits of Poetry* (New York: Alan Swallow, 1948), p. x.

82. Blackmur, "A Burden for Critics," p. 206.

83. Blackmur, "The Lion and the Honeycomb," *The Lion and the Honeycomb*, p. 184.

84. John Crowe Ransom, "Mr. Tate and the Professors," *Kenyon Review*, II (1940), 349.

85. John Crowe Ransom, *The New Criticism* (Norfolk, Conn.: New Directions, 1941), p. 139.

86. John Crowe Ransom, "The Literary Criticism of Aristotle," in *Lectures in Criticism*, ed. Huntington Cairns (New York: Pantheon, 1949), p. 17.

87. W. K. Wimsatt, Jr., "Poetry and Christian Thinking," *The Verbal Icon* (Lexington: University of Kentucky Press, 1954), p. 276.

9. LITERATURE AND THE LITERARY ESSAY

1. Henri Peyre, *Writers and Their Critics* (Ithaca, N. Y.: Cornell University Press, 1944), p. 305.

2. Stanley Edgar Hyman, *The Armed Vision* (New York: Knopf, 1948), p. 301.

3. Harry Levin in *The New Republic*, CIII (December 23, 1940), 906.

4. Robert W. Stallman, "The New Criticism and the Southern Critics," *A Southern Vanguard*, ed. Allen Tate (New York: Prentice-Hall, 1947), p. 45.

5. C. Hugh Holman, "The Defense of Art: Criticism Since 1930," *The Development of American Literary Criticism*, ed. Floyd Stovall (Chapel Hill: University of North Carolina Press, 1955), pp. 232, 234.

6. Hyman, *The Armed Vision*, p. 301.

7. John Edward Hardy, "The Achievement of Cleanth Brooks," *The Hopkins Review*, VI (1953), 160–61.

8. Leslie Fiedler, "Toward an Amateur Criticism," *Kenyon Review*, XII (1950), 572. Blackmur thinks of criticism as the "formal" discourse of the amateur "A Critic's Job of Work," *Language as Gesture* (New York: Harcourt, Brace, 1952), p. 372. The dilettante not at home but behind the lectern.

9. R. P. Blackmur, "W. B. Yeats: Between Myth and Philosophy," *Language as Gesture*, p. 111.

10. R. P. Blackmur, a contribution to "The Situation of American Writing," *The Partisan Reader* (New York: Dial, 1946), p. 600.

11. Elder Olson, "An Outline of Poetic Criticism," *Critics and Criticism*, ed. R. S. Crane (Chicago: University of Chicago Press, 1952), p. 556.

12. Norman MacLean, "Episode, Scene, Speech, and Word: The Madness of Lear," *ibid.*, p. 608.

Index